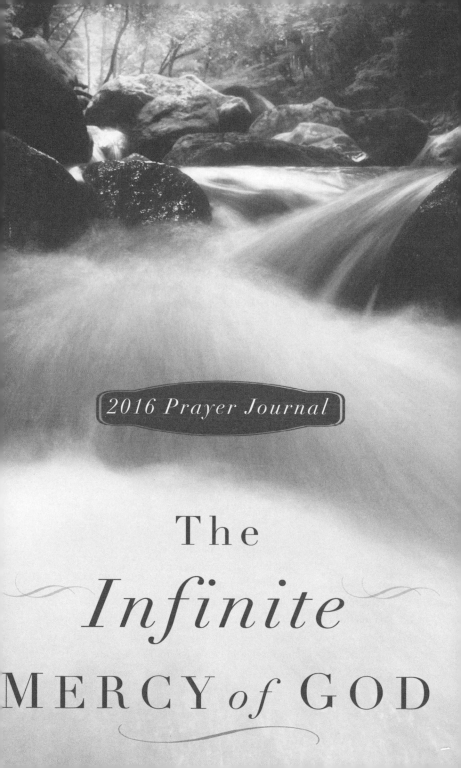

2016 Prayer Journal

The
Infinite
MERCY *of* GOD

The Word Among Us Press
7115 Guilford Drive, Suite 100
Frederick, Maryland 21704
www.wordamongus.org

ISBN: 978-1-59325-276-2

Scripture readings from the Roman Catholic liturgical calendar are adapted for
use in the United States. Celebrations of solemnities, feasts, memorials, or other
observances particular to your country, diocese, or parish may
result in some variation.

Compiled by Jeanne Kun

Cover design by John M. Lucas
Inside design by Andrea Alvarez

Printed in China

Dear Friend in Christ,

Only a few days after his election in 2013, Pope Francis noted, "Jesus has this message for us: mercy. I think—and I say it with humility—that this is the Lord's most powerful message: mercy." Since then, the Holy Father has repeatedly—indeed, almost unceasingly—reminded us of God's compassion and patience. Over and over again, he encourages us not to hesitate to ask the Lord for his help and forgiveness because he is always ready to show mercy to us sinners. So it is fitting that we have chosen "The Infinite Mercy of God" as the theme for the *2016 Prayer Journal.*

At the beginning of each month and at the top of each page of the journal, you'll find a Scripture verse or quotation from a saint, spiritual writer, or Church document. Most of these selections—including numerous ones from Pope Francis—speak of the mercy of God. So as you come before the Lord each day in prayer, open your heart to his grace and compassion, his favors and blessings, and his pardon—all signs of his unfailing mercy!

You'll also find ample space for journaling, a useful spiritual and practical tool to record your daily encounters with the Lord. You might find it helpful to make a note of Scripture passages that seem to speak particularly to you or jot down those circumstances in your life that you find challenging as well as those instances when you experience a "victory" or a special blessing from the Lord. Or perhaps you'd like to summarize what you learn in your times of quiet meditation, record resolutions you make in response to God's word to you, or keep track of petitions and answered prayers. At the end of the year, you'll have a convenient record that you can leaf through to help you recall how the Lord has worked in your life and what he has spoken to you.

Day after day, week after week, month after month, "let us not forget that the Lord always watches over us with mercy; he always watches over us with mercy. Let us not be afraid of approaching him" (Pope Francis).

The Word Among Us Press

Abbreviations of
Books of the Bible

Acts • Acts of the Apostles

Am • Amos

Bar • Baruch

1 Chr • 1 Chronicles

2 Chr • 2 Chronicles

Col • Colossians

1 Cor • 1 Corinthians

2 Cor • 2 Corinthians

Dn • Daniel

Dt • Deuteronomy

Eccl • Ecclesiastes

Eph • Ephesians

Est • Esther

Ex • Exodus

Ez • Ezekiel

Ezr • Ezra

Gal • Galatians

Gn • Genesis

Hb • Habakkuk

Heb • Hebrews

Hg • Haggai

Hos • Hosea

Is • Isaiah

Jas • James

Jb • Job

Jdt • Judith

Jer • Jeremiah

Jgs • Judges

Jl • Joel

Jn • John

1 Jn • 1 John

2 Jn • 2 John

3 Jn • 3 John

Jon • Jonah

Jos • Joshua

Jude • Jude

1 Kgs • 1 Kings

2 Kgs • 2 Kings

Lam • Lamentations

Lk • Luke

Lv • Leviticus

Mal • Malachi

1 Mc • 1 Maccabees

2 Mc • 2 Maccabees

Mi • Micah

Mk • Mark

Mt • Matthew

Na • Nahum

Neh • Nehemiah

Nm • Numbers

Ob • Obadiah

Phil • Philippians

Phlm • Philemon

Prv • Proverbs

Ps • Psalms

1 Pt • 1 Peter

2 Pt 2 Peter

Rom • Romans

Ru • Ruth

Rv • Revelation

Sg • Song of Songs

Sir • Sirach

1 Sm • 1 Samuel

2 Sm • 2 Samuel

Tb • Tobit

1 Thes • 1 Thessalonians

2 Thes • 2 Thessalonians

Ti • Titus

1 Tm • 1 Timothy

2 Tm • 2 Timothy

Wis • Wisdom

Zec • Zechariah

Zep • Zephaniah

JANUARY

S	M	T	W	T	F	S
					1	2
3	4	5	6	7	8	9
10	11	12	13	14	15	16
17	18	19	20	21	22	23
24	25	26	27	28	29	30
31						

FEBRUARY

S	M	T	W	T	F	S
	1	2	3	4	5	6
7	8	9	10	11	12	13
14	15	16	17	18	19	20
21	22	23	24	25	26	27
28	29					

MARCH

S	M	T	W	T	F	S
		1	2	3	4	5
6	7	8	9	10	11	12
13	14	15	16	17	18	19
20	21	22	23	24	25	26
27	28	29	30	31		

APRIL

S	M	T	W	T	F	S
					1	2
3	4	5	6	7	8	9
10	11	12	13	14	15	16
17	18	19	20	21	22	23
24	25	26	27	28	29	30

MAY

S	M	T	W	T	F	S
1	2	3	4	5	6	7
8	9	10	11	12	13	14
15	16	17	18	19	20	21
22	23	24	25	26	27	28
29	30	31				

JUNE

S	M	T	W	T	F	S
			1	2	3	4
5	6	7	8	9	10	11
12	13	14	15	16	17	18
19	20	21	22	23	24	25
26	27	28	29	30		

JULY

S	M	T	W	T	F	S
					1	2
3	4	5	6	7	8	9
10	11	12	13	14	15	16
17	18	19	20	21	22	23
24	25	26	27	28	29	30
31						

AUGUST

S	M	T	W	T	F	S
	1	2	3	4	5	6
7	8	9	10	11	12	13
14	15	16	17	18	19	20
21	22	23	24	25	26	27
28	29	30	31			

SEPTEMBER

S	M	T	W	T	F	S
				1	2	3
4	5	6	7	8	9	10
11	12	13	14	15	16	1/
18	19	20	21	22	23	24
25	26	27	28	29	30	

OCTOBER

S	M	T	W	T	F	S
						1
2	3	4	5	6	7	8
9	10	11	12	13	14	15
16	17	18	19	20	21	22
23	24	25	26	27	28	29
30	31					

NOVEMBER

S	M	T	W	T	F	S
		1	2	3	4	5
6	7	8	9	10	11	12
13	14	15	16	17	18	19
20	21	22	23	24	25	26
27	28	29	30			

DECEMBER

S	M	T	W	T	F	S
				1	2	3
4	5	6	7	8	9	10
11	12	13	14	15	16	17
18	19	20	21	22	23	24
25	26	27	28	29	30	31

JANUARY

Sun	Mon	Tue	Wed	Thu	Fri	Sat
					1	2
3	4	5	6	7	8	9
10	11	12	13	14	15	16
17	18	19	20	21	22	23
24	25	26	27	28	29	30
31						

God's face is the face of a merciful father who is always patient. Have you thought about God's patience, the patience he has with each one of us? That is his mercy. *He always* has patience, patience with us; he understands us, *he waits* for us, he does not tire of forgiving us if we are able to return to him with a contrite heart.

—*Pope Francis, Angelus Address, St. Peter's Square, March 17, 2013*

> May Mary, the Mother of God and our tender Mother,
> support us always, that we may remain faithful to
> our Christian vocation.
>
> —Pope Francis

. . . .

1
friday

SOLEMNITY OF MARY, THE HOLY MOTHER OF GOD
Nm 6:22-27 • Ps 67:2-3, 5-6, 8 • Gal 4:4-7 • Lk 2:16-21
Holy Day of Obligation

_____

_____

_____

_____

_____

_____

_____

_____

_____

SAINTS BASIL THE GREAT AND GREGORY NAZIANZEN
1 Jn 2:22-28 • Ps 98:1-4 • Jn 1:19-28

2
saturday

_____

_____

_____

_____

_____

_____

_____

_____

_____

_____

. . . .

Let us follow the star of inspiration and divine attraction which calls us to the crib, and let us go there to adore and love the Child Jesus and offer ourselves to him.

—St. Jane Frances de Chantal

3
sunday

THE EPIPHANY OF THE LORD
Is 60:1-6 • Ps 72:1-2, 7-8, 10-13 • Eph 3:2-3a, 5-6
Mt 2:1-12

_____
_____
_____
_____
_____
_____
_____
_____
_____

SAINT ELIZABETH ANN SETON
1 Jn 3:22—4:6 • Ps 2:7bc-8, 10-12a • Mt 4:12-17,
23-25

4
monday

_____
_____
_____
_____
_____
_____
_____
_____
_____

January

> The love which Our Lord had during his passion
> puts into full light God's love for us.
>
> —St. André Bessette

- -

5
tuesday

SAINT JOHN NEUMANN
1 Jn 4:7-10 • Ps 72:1-4, 7-8 • Mk 6:34-44

_____

_____

_____

_____

_____

_____

_____

_____

_____

SAINT ANDRÉ BESSETTE
1 Jn 4:11-18 • Ps 72:1-2, 10, 12-13 • Mk 6:45-52

6
wednesday

_____

_____

_____

_____

_____

_____

_____

_____

_____

_____

> Jesus is never far from us sinners. He wants to pour
> out on us, without limit, all of his mercy.
>
> —Pope Francis

7
thursday

SAINT RAYMOND OF PENYAFORT
1 Jn 4:19–5:4 • Ps 72:1-2, 14-15, 17 • Lk 4:14-22a

_____
_____
_____
_____
_____
_____
_____
_____
_____
_____

1 Jn 5:5-13 • Ps 147:12-15, 19-20 • Lk 5:12-16

8
friday

_____
_____
_____
_____
_____
_____
_____
_____
_____
_____

January

The baptism of Jesus is on his part the acceptance and inauguration of his mission as God's suffering Servant.
—*Catechism of the Catholic Church*, 536

9
saturday

1 Jn 5:14-21 • Ps 149:1-6a, 9b • Jn 3:22-30

_____
_____
_____
_____
_____
_____
_____
_____
_____

THE BAPTISM OF THE LORD

10
sunday

Is 42:1-4, 6-7 or Is 40:1-5, 9-11 • Ps 29:1-4, 9-10 or
Ps 104:1b-4, 24-25, 27-30• Acts 10:34-38 or
Ti 2:11-14; 3:4-7 • Lk 3:15-16, 21-22

_____
_____
_____
_____
_____
_____
_____
_____
_____

O Jesus, sure joy of my soul,
give me but a true love of you.
Let me seek you as my only good.

—Blessed Teresa of Calcutta

11
monday

1 Sm 1:1-8 • Ps 116:12-19 • Mk 1:14-20

_____
_____
_____
_____
_____
_____
_____
_____
_____
_____

1 Sm 1:9-20 • (Ps) 1 Sm 2:1, 4-8 • Mk 1:21-28

12
tuesday

_____
_____
_____
_____
_____
_____
_____
_____
_____
_____

January

> O God, may all my thoughts and words speak of you. . . .
> Breathe your Spirit into my faith and the way I confess it.
>
> —St. Hilary

13
wednesday

SAINT HILARY
1 Sm 3:1-10, 19-20 • Ps 40:2, 5, 7-10 • Mk 1:29-39

1 Sm 4:1-11 • Ps 44:10-11, 14-15, 24-25
Mk 1:40-45

14
thursday

> I will sing of your steadfast love, O LORD, forever, / with my mouth I will proclaim your faithfulness to all generations.
>
> —Psalm 89:1

15 friday

1 Sm 8:4-7, 10-22a • Ps 89:16-19 • Mk 2:1-12

1 Sm 9:1-4, 17-19; 10:1a • Ps 21:2-7 • Mk 2:13-17

16 saturday

January

You don't need to wallow in guilt.
Wallow in the mercy of God.

—St. John Vianney

SECOND SUNDAY IN ORDINARY TIME
Is 62:1-5 • Ps 96:1-3, 7-10 • 1 Cor 12:4-11
Jn 2:1-11

_____

_____

_____

_____

_____

_____

_____

_____

_____

_____

1 Sm 15:16-23 • Ps 50:8-9, 16b-17, 21, 23
Mk 2:18-22

_____

_____

_____

_____

_____

_____

_____

_____

_____

_____

> Let us not forget that the Lord always watches over us
> with mercy; he always watches over us with mercy.
> Let us not be afraid of approaching him!
>
> —Pope Francis

19 tuesday

1 Sm 16:1-13 • Ps 89:20-22, 27-28 • Mk 2:23-28

SAINT FABIAN; SAINT SEBASTIAN

1 Sm 17:32-33, 37, 40-51 • Ps 144:1b-2, 9-10
Mk 3:1-6

20 wednesday

January

The deepest element of God's commandment to protect
human life is the requirement to show reverence and love for
every person and the life of every person.

—St. John Paul II

21
thursday

SAINT AGNES
1 Sm 18:6-9; 19:1-7 • Ps 56:2-3, 9-13 • Mk 3:7-12

_____
_____
_____
_____
_____
_____
_____
_____
_____
_____

**DAY OF PRAYER FOR THE LEGAL
PROTECTION OF UNBORN CHILDREN**
1 Sm 24:3-21 • Ps 57:2-4, 6, 11 • Mk 3:13-19

22
friday

_____
_____
_____
_____
_____
_____
_____
_____
_____
_____

> Lord, have mercy on me! . . . I make no effort to conceal my wounds. You are my physician, I your patient. You are merciful; I stand in need of mercy.
>
> —St. Augustine

23
saturday

SAINT VINCENT; SAINT MARIANNE COPE
2 Sm 1:1-4, 11-12, 19, 23-27 • Ps 80:2-3, 5-7
Mk 3:20-21

_____
_____
_____
_____
_____
_____
_____
_____
_____
_____

THIRD SUNDAY IN ORDINARY TIME
Neh 8:2-4a, 5-6, 8-10 • Ps 19:8-10, 15 • 1 Cor 12:12-30 • Lk 1:1-4; 4:14-21

24
sunday

_____
_____
_____
_____
_____
_____
_____
_____
_____
_____
_____

January

> [God] saved us, not because of deeds done by us in righteousness, but in virtue of his own mercy, by the washing of regeneration and renewal in the Holy Spirit.
>
> —Titus 3:5

25
monday

THE CONVERSION OF SAINT PAUL THE APOSTLE
Acts 22:3-16 or Acts 9:1-22 • Ps 117:1b-2
Mk 16:15-18

SAINTS TIMOTHY AND TITUS
2 Tm 1:1-8 or Ti 1:1-5 • Ps 96:1-3, 7-8a, 10
Mk 3:31-35

26
tuesday

27
wednesday

SAINT ANGELA MERICI
2 Sm 7:4-17 • Ps 89:4-5, 27-30 • Mk 4:1-20

_____
_____
_____
_____
_____
_____
_____
_____
_____
_____

SAINT THOMAS AQUINAS
2 Sm 7:18-19, 24-29 • Ps 132:1-5, 11-14
Mk 4:21-25

28
thursday

_____
_____
_____
_____
_____
_____
_____
_____
_____
_____

January

> What tenderness there is in Jesus' love for man!
> In his infinite goodness, he established, with each of us,
> bonds of sublime love! His love has no limits!
>
> —St. John Bosco

29
friday

2 Sm 11:1-4a, 5-10a, 13-17 • Ps 51:3-7, 10-11
Mk 4:26-34

_____
_____
_____
_____
_____
_____
_____
_____
_____
_____

SAINT JOHN BOSCO
2 Sm 12:1-7a, 10-17 • Ps 51:12-17 • Mk 4:35-41

30
saturday

_____
_____
_____
_____
_____
_____
_____
_____
_____
_____

Heaven and earth may change,
but God's mercy will never be exhausted.

—St. Faustina Kowalska

31
sunday

FOURTH SUNDAY IN ORDINARY TIME
Jer 1:4-5, 17-19 • Ps 71:1-6, 15-17 • 1 Cor 12:31–
13:13 • Lk 4:21-30

January

FEBRUARY

Sun	Mon	Tue	Wed	Thu	Fri	Sat
	1	2	3	4	5	6
7	8	9	10	11	12	13
14	15	16	17	18	19	20
21	22	23	24	25	26	27
28	29					

O Lord, my trust is in your

mercies, of which there is no end.

Look, therefore, on me with eyes

of your mercy, O Lord Jesus Christ, God

and man. *Hear me,* whose trust

is in you: upon me, mercy! —who am

full of misery and sin.

—*St. Ambrose*

> We, too, may look for the great grace that was granted
> Simeon. He has shown us how to prepare for and merit it.
> The desire of our hearts should be to see Jesus.
>
> —Edward Leen, CSSp

1
monday

2 Sm 15:13-14, 30; 16:5-13 • Ps 3:2-7 • Mk 5:1-20

_____

_____

_____

_____

_____

_____

_____

_____

_____

_____

THE PRESENTATION OF THE LORD
Mal 3:1-4 • Ps 24:7-10 • Heb 2:14-18 • Lk 2:22-40

2
tuesday

_____

_____

_____

_____

_____

_____

_____

_____

_____

_____

Let me fall into the hand of the LORD,
for his mercy is very great.

—1 Chronicles 21:13

---

3 wednesday

SAINT BLAISE; SAINT ANSGAR
2 Sm 24:2, 9-17 • Ps 32:1-2, 5-7 • Mk 6:1-6

_____
_____
_____
_____
_____
_____
_____
_____
_____
_____

1 Kgs 2:1-4, 10-12 • (Ps) 1 Chr 29:10-12 • Mk 6:7-13

4 thursday

_____
_____
_____
_____
_____
_____
_____
_____
_____
_____
_____

February

Jesus Christ, Lord of all, you see my heart,
you know my desires. You alone possess all that I am.

—St. Agatha

SAINT AGATHA

5 friday

Sir 47:2-11 • Ps 18:31, 47, 50-51 • Mk 6:14-29

_____

_____

_____

_____

_____

_____

_____

_____

_____

SAINT PAUL MIKI AND COMPANIONS

1 Kgs 3:4-13 • Ps 119:9-14 • Mk 6:30-34

6 saturday

_____

_____

_____

_____

_____

_____

_____

_____

_____

> I have given everything to my Master: He will take care of me. . . . The best thing for us is not what we consider best, but what the Lord wants of us!
>
> —St. Josephine Bakhita

7
sunday

FIFTH SUNDAY IN ORDINARY TIME
Is 6:1-2a, 3-8 • Ps 138:1-5, 7-8 • 1 Cor 15:1-11
Lk 5:1-11

_____
_____
_____
_____
_____
_____
_____
_____
_____
_____

SAINT JEROME EMILIANI;
SAINT JOSPEHINE BAKHITA
1 Kgs 8:1-7, 9-13 • Ps 132:6-10 • Mk 6:53-56

8
monday

_____
_____
_____
_____
_____
_____
_____
_____
_____
_____

February

> Let us give thanks to God for the mystery of his crucified love;
> authentic faith, conversion, and openness of heart to the brethren:
> these are the essential elements for living the season of Lent.
>
> —Pope Francis

9 tuesday

1 Kgs 8:22-23, 27-30 • Ps 84:3-5, 10-11 • Mk 7:1-13

ASH WEDNESDAY

Jl 2:12-18 • Ps 51:3-6b, 12-14, 17 • 2 Cor 5:20—6:2
Mt 6:1-6, 16-18

10 wednesday

Ask Mary to lead you to Jesus and you will
know what it is to live by his side.

—Cardinal Francis Xavier Nguyen Van Thuan

11 thursday

OUR LADY OF LOURDES
Dt 30:15-20 • Ps 1:1-4, 6 • Lk 9:22-25

Is 58:1-9a • Ps 51:3-6b, 18-19 • Mt 9:14-15

12 friday

February

I urge you to find in this Lenten season prolonged
moments of silence . . . in order to review your own lives in
the light of the loving plan of the heavenly Father.

—Pope Benedict XVI

13
saturday

Is 58:9b-14 • Ps 86:1-6 • Lk 5:27-32

_____
_____
_____
_____
_____
_____
_____
_____
_____

FIRST SUNDAY OF LENT
Dt 26:4-10 • Ps 91:1-2, 10-15 • Rom 10:8-13
Lk 4:1-13

14
sunday

_____
_____
_____
_____
_____
_____
_____
_____
_____

The LORD is near to the brokenhearted, /
and saves the crushed in spirit.

—Psalm 34:18

. . . .

15
monday

Lv 19:1-2, 11-18 • Ps 19:8-10, 15 • Mt 25:31-46

_____

_____

_____

_____

_____

_____

_____

_____

_____

Is 55:10-11 • Ps 34:4-7, 16-19 • Mt 6:7-15

16
tuesday

_____

_____

_____

_____

_____

_____

_____

_____

_____

February

. . . .

> Have mercy on me, O God, / according to your
> steadfast love; / according to your abundant mercy /
> blot out my transgressions.
>
> —Psalm 51:1

17 wednesday
THE SEVEN HOLY FOUNDERS OF THE SERVITE ORDER
Jon 3:1-10 • Ps 51:3-4, 12-13, 18-19 • Lk 11:29-32

Est C:12, 14-16, 23-25 • Ps 138:1-3, 7c-8 • Mt 7:7-12

18 thursday

During Lent let us improve our spirit of prayer and
recollection. Let us free our minds from all that is not Jesus.

—Blessed Teresa of Calcutta

19
friday

Ez 18:21-28 • Ps 130:1-8 • Mt 5:20-26

_____

_____

_____

_____

_____

_____

_____

_____

_____

_____

Dt 26:16-19 • Ps 119:1-2, 4-5, 7-8 • Mt 5:43-48

20
saturday

_____

_____

_____

_____

_____

_____

_____

_____

_____

_____

February

[Jesus said to his disciples:] "Be merciful,
just as your Father is merciful."

—Luke 6:36

- -

21
sunday

SECOND SUNDAY OF LENT
Gn 15:5-12, 17-18 • Ps 27:1, 7-9, 13-14 • Phil 3:17–
4:1 • Lk 9:28b-36

_____

_____

_____

_____

_____

_____

_____

_____

_____

_____

THE CHAIR OF SAINT PETER THE APOSTLE
1 Pt 5:1-4 • Ps 23:1-6 • Mt 16:13-19

22
monday

_____

_____

_____

_____

_____

_____

_____

_____

_____

_____

Help one another with the generosity of the Lord,
and despise no one. When you have the opportunity
to do good, do not let it go by.

—St. Polycarp

23
tuesday

SAINT POLYCARP
Is 1:10, 16-20 • Ps 50:8-9, 16b-17, 21, 23
Mt 23:1-12

Jer 18:18-20 • Ps 31:5-6, 14-16 • Mt 20:17-28

24
wednesday

February

25 thursday

Jer 17:5-10 • Ps 1:1-4, 6 • Lk 16:19-31

_____
_____
_____
_____
_____
_____
_____
_____
_____

Gn 37:3-4, 12-13a, 17b-28a • Ps 105:16-21
Mt 21:33-43, 45-46

26 friday

_____
_____
_____
_____
_____
_____
_____
_____
_____
_____

My eyes are always on the Lord, for he rescues my feet
from the snare. Turn to me and have mercy on me,
for I am alone and poor (cf. Psalm 25:15-16).

—Entrance Antiphon, Third Sunday of Lent

27
saturday

Mi 7:14-15, 18-20 • Ps 103:1-4, 9-12 • Lk 15:1-3,
11-32

_____
_____
_____
_____
_____
_____
_____
_____
_____
_____

THIRD SUNDAY OF LENT
Ex 3:1-8a, 13-15 • Ps 103:1-4, 6-8, 11 • 1 Cor 10:1-6,
10-12 • Lk 13:1-9

28
sunday

_____
_____
_____
_____
_____
_____
_____
_____
_____

February

Each year in preparation for Easter, Lent invites
us to follow Christ in the mystery of his prayer,
source of light and strength in time of trial.

—St. John Paul II

29
monday

2 Kgs 5:1-15b • Ps 42:2-3; 43:3-4 • Lk 4:24-30

Let us pray that our Lenten journey will strengthen
us in the struggle against all forms of temptation.

—Pope Benedict XVI

February

MARCH

Sun	Mon	Tue	Wed	Thu	Fri	Sat
		1	2	3	4	5
6	7	8	9	10	11	12
13	14	15	16	17	18	19
20	21	22	23	24	25	26
27	28	29	30	31		

What heart can describe the heart of the divine mercy? *What mind* is not amazed by the riches of such great love? . . . Let us consider with how much *goodness* God puts up with us, let us bear in mind the depth of his love. He is not only lenient toward our sins, but he even *promises* the heavenly kingdom to those who repent after sinning. Let each of us say from the very depths of our hearts, let us all say, *My God, my mercy.*

—*St. Gregory the Great*

Lent is a "powerful" season, a turning point
that can foster change and conversion in each of us.
We all need to improve, to change for the better.

—Pope Francis

- -

1
tuesday

Dn 3:25, 34-43 • Ps 25:4-9 • Mt 18:21-35

_____

_____

_____

_____

_____

_____

_____

_____

_____

_____

Dt 4:1, 5-9 • Ps 147:12-13, 15-16, 19-20 • Mt 5:17-19

2
wednesday

_____

_____

_____

_____

_____

_____

_____

_____

_____

Christ may be leading me out to a cross. If so, I can have no
hesitation about following him. I must follow him closely, so
that . . . I shall be near him, my Good Shepherd.

—St. Katharine Drexel

3 thursday

SAINT KATHARINE DREXEL
Jer 7:23-28 • Ps 95:1-2, 6-9 • Lk 11:14-23

SAINT CASIMIR
Hos 14:2-10 • Ps 81:6c-11b, 14, 17 • Mk 12:28-34

4 friday

March

The tax collector, standing far off, would not even look up to heaven, but was beating his breast and saying, "God, be merciful me, a sinner!"

—Luke 18:13

5 saturday

Hos 6:1-6 • Ps 51:3-4, 18-21b • Lk 18:9-14

_____

_____

_____

_____

_____

_____

_____

_____

_____

FOURTH SUNDAY OF LENT

Jos 5:9a, 10-12 • Ps 34:2-7 • 2 Cor 5:17-21
Lk 15:1-3, 11-32

6 sunday

_____

_____

_____

_____

_____

_____

_____

_____

_____

_____

> When you feel depressed, reflect on the passion of
> Our Lord Jesus Christ and his precious wounds, and you
> will experience great consolation.
>
> —St. John of God

7
monday

SAINTS PERPETUA AND FELICITY
Is 65:17-21 • Ps 30:2, 4-6, 11-13b • Jn 4:43-54

_____
_____
_____
_____
_____
_____
_____
_____
_____
_____

SAINT JOHN OF GOD
Ez 47:1-9, 12 • Ps 46:2-3, 5-6, 8-9 • Jn 5:1-16

8
tuesday

_____
_____
_____
_____
_____
_____
_____
_____
_____
_____

March

Hope everything from the mercy of God.
It is as boundless as his power.

—St. Frances of Rome

9
wednesday

SAINT FRANCES OF ROME
Is 49:8-15 • Ps 145:8-9, 13c-14, 17-18 • Jn 5:17-30

Ex 32:7-14 • Ps 106:19-23 • Jn 5:31-47

10
thursday

Each year Lent . . . stimulates us to rediscover the mercy
of God so that we, in turn, become more merciful toward
our brothers and sisters.

—Pope Benedict XVI

11
friday

Wis 2:1a, 12-22 • Ps 34:17-21, 23 • Jn 7:1-2, 10,
25-30

_____
_____
_____
_____
_____
_____
_____
_____
_____
_____

Jer 11:18-20 • Ps 7:2-3, 9b-12 • Jn 7:40-53

12
saturday

_____
_____
_____
_____
_____
_____
_____
_____
_____

March

Lord, you are the source of unfailing light. Give us true knowledge of your mercy so that we may renounce our pride and be filled with the riches of your house.

—Psalm Prayer in Fifth Week of Lent, *Liturgy of the Hours*

13
sunday

FIFTH SUNDAY OF LENT
Is 43:16-21 • Ps 126:1-6 • Phil 3:8-14 • Jn 8:1-11

Dn 13:1-9, 15-17, 19-30, 33-62 • Ps 23:1-6
Jn 8:12-20

14
monday

O LORD, do not put us to shame, but deal with us in your
patience and in your abundant mercy.

—Daniel 3:42

15
tuesday

Nm 21:4-9 • Ps 102:2-3, 16-21 • Jn 8:21-30

_____
_____
_____
_____
_____
_____
_____
_____
_____
_____

Dn 3:14-20, 91-92, 95 • (Ps) Dn 3:52-56 • Jn 8:31-42

16
wednesday

_____
_____
_____
_____
_____
_____
_____
_____
_____
_____

March

Turn trustingly to the Lord who is my God. Put your faith in him with all your heart, because nothing is impossible to him.

—St. Patrick

17
thursday

SAINT PATRICK
Gn 17:3-9 • Ps 105:4-9 • Jn 8:51-59

_____
_____
_____
_____
_____
_____
_____
_____
_____
_____

SAINT CYRIL OF JERUSALEM
Jer 20:10-13 • Ps 18:2-7 • Jn 10:31-42

18
friday

_____
_____
_____
_____
_____
_____
_____
_____
_____
_____

> Living Holy Week means entering ever more deeply into the logic of God, into the logic of the cross, which is not primarily that of suffering and death, but rather that of love and of the gift of self which brings life.
>
> —Pope Francis

19
saturday

SAINT JOSEPH, SPOUSE OF THE BLESSED VIRGIN MARY

2 Sm 7:4-5a, 12-14a, 16 • Ps 89:2-5, 27, 29 • Rom 4:13, 16-18, 22 • Mt 1:16, 18-21, 24a or Lk 2:41-51a

PALM SUNDAY OF THE PASSION OF THE LORD

Lk 19:28-40 • Is 50:4-7 • Ps 22:8-9, 17-20, 23-24
Phil 2:6-11 • Lk 22:14–23:56

20
sunday

March

. . . .

21
monday

MONDAY OF HOLY WEEK
Is 42:1-7 • Ps 27:1-3, 13-14 • Jn 12:1-11

_____

_____

_____

_____

_____

_____

_____

_____

_____

_____

TUESDAY OF HOLY WEEK
Is 49:1-6 • Ps 71:1-6b, 15, 17 • Jn 13:21-33, 36-38

22
tuesday

_____

_____

_____

_____

_____

_____

_____

_____

_____

_____

God is a crucified God. God is the God who allows himself to be defeated; God is the God who has revealed himself in the poor. God is the God who has washed my feet.

—Carlo Carretto

23 wednesday

WEDNESDAY OF HOLY WEEK
Is 50:4-9a • Ps 69:8-10, 21-22, 31, 33-34
Mt 26:14-25

HOLY THURSDAY
Ex 12:1-8, 11-14 • Ps 116:12-13, 15-18
1 Cor 11:23-26 • Jn 13:1-15

24 thursday

March

> The cross, even after the resurrection of the Son of God, . . . never ceases to speak of God the Father, who is absolutely faithful to his eternal love for man.
>
> —St. John Paul II

25 friday

FRIDAY OF THE PASSION OF THE LORD (GOOD FRIDAY)

Is 52:13–53:12 • Ps 31:2, 6, 12-13, 15-17, 25
Heb 4:14-16; 5:7-9 • Jn 18:1–19:42

HOLY SATURDAY (EASTER VIGIL)

Gn 1:1–2:2 • Gn 22:1-18 • Ex 14:15–15:1
Is 54:5-14 • Is 55:1-11 • Bar 3:9-15, 32–4:4
Ez 36:16-17a, 18-28 • Rom 6:3-11 • Ps 118:1-2,
16-17, 22-23 • Lk 24:1-12

26 saturday

> By resurrecting Jesus from the dead, God transformed
> our greatest sins into his greatest mercy.
>
> —Raniero Cantalamessa, OFM Cap

27
sunday

EASTER SUNDAY OF THE RESURRECTION OF THE LORD

Acts 10:34a, 37-43 • Ps 118:1-2, 16-17, 22-23
Col 3:1-4 or 1 Cor 5:6b-8 • Jn 20:1-9 or Lk 24:1-12
or at an afternoon or evening Mass, Lk 24:13-35

MONDAY WITHIN THE OCTAVE OF EASTER

Acts 2:14, 22-33 • Ps 16:1-2a, 5, 7-11 • Mt 28:8-15

28
monday

March

Jesus is risen; there is hope for you, you are no longer in the power of sin, of evil! Love has triumphed, mercy has been victorious! The mercy of God always triumphs!

—Pope Francis

29
tuesday

TUESDAY WITHIN THE OCTAVE OF EASTER
Acts 2:36-41 • Ps 33:4-5, 18-20, 22 • Jn 20:11-18

_____
_____
_____
_____
_____
_____
_____
_____
_____

TUESDAY WITHIN THE OCTAVE OF EASTER
Acts 3:1-10 • Ps 105:1-4, 6-9 • Lk 24:13-35

30
wednesday

_____
_____
_____
_____
_____
_____
_____
_____
_____

We Need Your Help!

Dear Friend in Christ,

   Below is a survey form to help us know how to best meet your needs and interests in future editions of the *Prayer Journal.* Please take a moment and answer the following questions. In gratitude for your completed survey, we will take 10% off the price of your *Prayer Journal* for the next year!

1) In your use of the *Prayer Journal,* what features are essential to you? (Check as many responses as you find relevant and/or important to you personally.)

☐ The daily Mass readings citations

☐ Designation of special holy days and saints' feast days

☐ Referencing the day of the week and the date of the month

☐ Inspiring spiritual quotation on each page

☐ Spiral binding

2) The *Prayer Journal's* particular theme for the year (this year it is "The Infinite Mercy of God") is an important factor in my decision to purchase it.

☐ Agree. The year's theme is important in my purchasing decision.

☐ Disagree. The year's theme has little impact on my purchasing decision.

3) Which of the above features listed in question #1 would you miss if they were not included in the journal?

_____

_____

4) Do you have any suggestions for improving the *Prayer Journal?*

_____

_____

5) Do you use the *Prayer Journal's* companion book, called *Abide in My Word: Mass Readings at Your Fingertips?*

☐ Yes   ☐ No

Thank you for completing our survey. To reserve next year's *Prayer Journal* at the reduced price, complete the form below and return to:

Prayer Journal Survey
The Word Among Us
7115 Guilford Drive, Suite 100
Frederick, MD 21704

Quantities Limited! Reserve your copy now and save 10%
Order 2 or more copies and save 20% !

☐ **YES!** Reserve _____ copies of the *2017 Prayer Journal*. JP2017
(1 @ $12.56; 2 or more @ $11.16 each plus shipping and handling)

☐ **YES!** Reserve _____ copies of *Abide in My Word 2017*. AB2017
(1 *Abide in My Word* @ $14.85; 2 or more @ $13.20 each plus shipping and handling)

☐ **YES!** Reserve the *2017 Prayer Journal* **AND** *2017 Abide in My Word* for only $24.36 plus shipping and handling! 17SETA

I will not be billed until I receive my *Prayer Journal* or *Abide in My Word* in the fall of 2016.

Name _____

Address _____

City _____

State _____ Zip _____

Country _____

Phone (_____) _____

E-mail _____

NOTE: Only surveys returned by <u>May 31, 2016</u>, will be eligible for this discount.

QUESTIONS?
Call *The Word Among Us* Customer Service at 1-800-775-WORD (9673) if you have any questions about this discount offer.

SHIPPING & HANDLING (Add to total product order):					
If your subtotal is:	$0-15	$16-$35	$36-50	$51-75	$76-100
Add shipping of:	$5	$7	$9	$11	$13

CPPJ16S

Easter is a feast of joy—the joy of the Lord. Let nothing so disturb us, so fill us with sorrow or discouragement, as to make us forfeit the joy of the resurrection.

—Blessed Teresa of Calcutta

31
thursday

THURSDAY WITHIN THE OCTAVE OF EASTER
Acts 3:11-26 • Ps 8:2, 5-9 • Lk 24:35-48

March

APRIL

Sun	Mon	Tue	Wed	Thu	Fri	Sat
					1	2
3	4	5	6	7	8	9
10	11	12	13	14	15	16
17	18	19	20	21	22	23
24	25	26	27	28	29	30

Pardon me, *O Mercy* of my God,

for having despised so long your mercy's voice!

In deep sorrow and contrition,

I cast myself at your feet:

have mercy on me.

Amen.

—*St. Ignatius of Loyola*

> Rich is the mercy of our God, and abundantly does he bestow grace upon grace on those who love him.
>
> —St. Elizabeth of Schönau

1 friday
FRIDAY WITHIN THE OCTAVE OF EASTER
Acts 4:1-12 • Ps 118:1-2, 4, 22-27a • Jn 21:1-14

SATURDAY WITHIN THE OCTAVE OF EASTER
Acts 4:13-21 • Ps 118:1, 14-21 • Mk 16:9-15

2 saturday

> Jesus has this message for us: mercy. . . .
> I say it with humility—that this is the Lord's most
> powerful message: mercy.
>
> —Pope Francis

. . . .

3
sunday

SECOND SUNDAY OF EASTER OR SUNDAY OF DIVINE MERCY
Acts 5:12-16 • Ps 118:2-4, 13-15, 22-24 • Rv 1:9-11a, 12-13, 17-19 • Jn 20:19-31

_____

_____

_____

_____

_____

_____

_____

_____

_____

THE ANNUNCIATION OF THE LORD
Is 7:10-14; 8:10 • Ps 40:7-11 • Heb 10:4-10
Lk 1:26-38

4
monday

_____

_____

_____

_____

_____

_____

_____

_____

_____

April

. . . .

Have mercy on me, O Lord, for I am weak: heal me, O Lord, for my bones are troubled. . . . Have mercy on me, O God, have mercy on me: for my soul trusts in you.

—St. Vincent Ferrer

5
tuesday

SAINT VINCENT FERRER
Acts 4:32-37 • Ps 93:1-2, 5 • Jn 3:7b-15

Acts 5:17-26 • Ps 34:2-9 • Jn 3:16-21

6
wednesday

Show your love for those whom God has given you,
just as Christ loved the Church.

—St. John Baptist de la Salle

7
thursday

SAINT JOHN BAPTIST DE LA SALLE
Acts 5:27-33 • Ps 34:2, 9, 17-20 • Jn 3:31-36

Acts 5:34-42 • Ps 27:1, 4, 13-14 • Jn 6:1-15

8
friday

April

May the joy and love of the risen Jesus be always with you, in you, and among you, so that we all become the true witnesses of his Father's love for the world.

—Blessed Teresa of Calcutta

9 saturday

Acts 6:1-7 • Ps 33:1-2, 4-5, 18-19 • Jn 6:16-21

_____
_____
_____
_____
_____
_____
_____
_____
_____

THIRD SUNDAY OF EASTER
Acts 5:27-32, 40b-41 • Ps 30:2, 4-6, 11-13
Rv 5:11-14 • Jn 21:1-19

10 sunday

_____
_____
_____
_____
_____
_____
_____
_____
_____

> Love above all else our merciful Father in heaven, and serve
> him with all your strength and purity of heart.
>
> —St. Francis of Paola

11
monday

SAINT STANISLAUS
Acts 6:8-15 • Ps 119:23-24, 26-27, 29-30 • Jn 6:22-29

_____
_____
_____
_____
_____
_____
_____
_____
_____
_____

Acts 7:51–8:1a • Ps 31:3c-4, 6-8a, 17, 21ab
Jn 6:30-35

12
tuesday

_____
_____
_____
_____
_____
_____
_____
_____
_____
_____

April

Blessed be God, / because he has not rejected my prayer / or removed his steadfast love from me.

—Psalm 66:20

13
wednesday

SAINT MARTIN I
Acts 8:1b-8 • Ps 66:1-3a, 4-7a • Jn 6:35-40

_____
_____
_____
_____
_____
_____
_____
_____
_____
_____

Acts 8:26-40 • Ps 66:8-9, 16-17, 20 • Jn 6:44-51

14
thursday

_____
_____
_____
_____
_____
_____
_____
_____
_____
_____

> Confession heals, confession justifies, confession grants
> pardon of sin. . . . In confession there is a chance for mercy.
> Believe it firmly. Hope and have confidence in confession.
>
> —St. Isidore

15 friday

Acts 9:1-20 • Ps 117:1b-2 • Jn 6:52-59

Acts 9:31-42 • Ps 116:12-17 • Jn 6:60-69

16 saturday

April

> Our belief in Christ's resurrection is the very heart of our faith, the basis of our hope in God's promises, and our trust in his victory over sin and death.
>
> —Pope Francis

17 sunday

FOURTH SUNDAY OF EASTER
Acts 13:14, 43-52 • Ps 100:1-3, 5 • Rv 7:9, 14b-17
Jn 10:27-30

_____
_____
_____
_____
_____
_____
_____
_____
_____
_____

Acts 11:1-18 • Ps 42:2-3; 43:3-4 • Jn 10:1-10

18 monday

_____
_____
_____
_____
_____
_____
_____
_____
_____
_____

Place all your hope in the heart of Jesus; it is a safe asylum; for he who trusts in God is sheltered and protected by his mercy.

—St. Bernard of Clairvaux

19
tuesday

Acts 11:19-26 • Ps 87:1b-7 • Jn 10:22-30

_____
_____
_____
_____
_____
_____
_____
_____
_____
_____

Acts 12:24–13:5a • Ps 67:2-3, 5-6, 8 • Jn 12:44-50

20
wednesday

_____
_____
_____
_____
_____
_____
_____
_____
_____
_____
_____

April

Speak now, my heart, and say to God,
"I seek your face; your face, Lord, I seek."

—St. Anselm

21
thursday

SAINT ANSELM
Acts 13:13-25 • Ps 89:2-3, 21-22, 25, 27
Jn 13:16-20

_____
_____
_____
_____
_____
_____
_____
_____
_____
_____

Acts 13:26-33 • Ps 2:6-11b • Jn 14:1-6

22
friday

_____
_____
_____
_____
_____
_____
_____
_____
_____
_____

We do pray for mercy; / And that same prayer doth teach us all to render the deeds of mercy.

—William Shakespeare

23
saturday

SAINT GEORGE; SAINT ADALBERT
Acts 13:44-52 • Ps 98:1-4 • Jn 14:7-14

_____
_____
_____
_____
_____
_____
_____
_____
_____
_____

FIFTH SUNDAY OF EASTER
Acts 14:21-27 • Ps 145:8-13 • Rv 21:1-5a • Jn 13:31-33a, 34-35

24
sunday

_____
_____
_____
_____
_____
_____
_____
_____
_____
_____

April

Learn from St. Mark to keep the image of the Son of Man
ever before your mind, and to ponder every syllable
which fell from his lips.

—Butler's Lives of the Saints

25 monday

SAINT MARK, EVANGELIST
1 Pt 5:5b-14 • Ps 89:2-3, 6-7, 16-17 • Mk 16:15-20

_____

_____

_____

_____

_____

_____

_____

_____

_____

_____

Acts 14:19-28 • Ps 145:10-13b, 21 • Jn 14:27-31a

26 tuesday

_____

_____

_____

_____

_____

_____

_____

_____

_____

_____

Jesus loves us. He does what he teaches.
He forgives his enemies. His teaching is good.

—St. Peter Chanel

27 wednesday

Acts 15:1-6 • Ps 122:1-5 • Jn 15:1-8

_____
_____
_____
_____
_____
_____
_____
_____
_____
_____

SAINT PETER CHANEL; SAINT LOUIS GRIGNION DE MONTFORT

Acts 15:7-21 • Ps 96:1-3, 10 • Jn 15:9-11

28 thursday

_____
_____
_____
_____
_____
_____
_____
_____
_____
_____

April

Every day you give us this food,
showing us yourself in the sacrament of the altar. . . .
And what has done this? Your mercy!

—St. Catherine of Siena

29
friday

SAINT CATHERINE OF SIENA
Acts 15:22-31 • Ps 57:8-10, 12 • Jn 15:12-17

_____
_____
_____
_____
_____
_____
_____
_____
_____
_____

SAINT PIUS V
Acts 16:1-10 • Ps 100:1b-3, 5 • Jn 15:18-21

30
saturday

_____
_____
_____
_____
_____
_____
_____
_____
_____
_____

It would be well if we were in the habit of looking at all we have as God's gift, undeservedly given, and day by day continued to us solely by his mercy. He gave; he may take away.

—Blessed John Henry Newman

April

MAY

Sun	Mon	Tue	Wed	Thu	Fri	Sat
1	2	3	4	5	6	7
8	9	10	11	12	13	14
15	16	17	18	19	20	21
22	23	24	25	26	27	28
29	30	31				

The Church lives an *authentic* life when she professes and proclaims mercy—the most *stupendous* attribute of the Creator and of the Redeemer—and when she brings people close to the sources of the Savior's mercy, of which she is the trustee and dispenser. Of great *significance* in this area is constant meditation on the Word of God, and above all conscious and mature *participation* in the Eucharist and in the sacrament of Penance or Reconciliation.

—*St. John Paul II,* Rich in Mercy, *13*

> [Jesus] has a merciful heart! If we show him our inner wounds, our inner sins, he will always forgive us. It is pure mercy. Let us go to Jesus!
>
> —Pope Francis

1 sunday

SIXTH SUNDAY OF EASTER
Acts 15:1-2, 22-29 • Ps 67:2-3, 5-6, 8 • Rv 21:10-14, 22-23 • Jn 14:23-29

_____
_____
_____
_____
_____
_____
_____
_____
_____
_____

SAINT ATHANASIUS
Acts 16:11-15 • Ps 149:1b-6a, 9b • Jn 15:26–16:4a

2 monday

_____
_____
_____
_____
_____
_____
_____
_____
_____
_____

> Like every good evangelist, Philip not only spoke to others
> about Christ but invited them to meet him personally.
>
> —Pope Benedict XVI

3
tuesday

SAINTS PHILIP AND JAMES, APOSTLES
1 Cor 15:1-8 • Ps 19:2-5 • Jn 14:6-14

_____
_____
_____
_____
_____
_____
_____
_____
_____
_____

Acts 17:15, 22–18:1 • Ps 148:1-2, 11-14 • Jn 16:12-15

4
wednesday

_____
_____
_____
_____
_____
_____
_____
_____
_____

May

> With Christ we have ascended, mystically, but also really, to the highest heavens, and have won through Christ a grace more wonderful than the one we had lost.
>
> —St. Leo the Great

5
thursday

Acts 18:1-8 • Ps 98:1, 4 • Jn 16:16-20
OR THE ASCENSION OF THE LORD
• Acts 1:1-11 • Ps 47:2-3, 6-9 • Eph 1:17-23 or
Heb 9:24-28; 10:19-23 • Lk 24:46-53

_____
_____
_____
_____
_____
_____
_____
_____
_____

Acts 18:9-18 • Ps 47:2-7 • Jn 16:20-23

6
friday

_____
_____
_____
_____
_____
_____
_____
_____
_____
_____

God our Father, make us joyful in the ascension of your Son
Jesus Christ. May we follow him into the new creation, for
his ascension is our glory and our hope.

—Ascension Evening Prayer, *Liturgy of the Hours*

7 saturday

Acts 18:23-28 • Ps 47:2-3, 8-10 • Jn 16:23b-28

_____
_____
_____
_____
_____
_____
_____
_____
_____

THE ASCENSION OF THE LORD

Acts 1:1-11 • Ps 47:2-3, 6-9 • Eph 1:17-23 or Heb 9:24-28;
10:19-23 • Lk 24:46-53 **OR SEVENTH SUNDAY OF
EASTER** • Acts 7:55-60 • Ps 97:1-2, 6-7, 9
Rv 22:12-14, 16-17, 20 • Jn 17:20-26

8 sunday

_____
_____
_____
_____
_____
_____
_____
_____
_____

May

> Remember always that God is eternal.
> Work courageously in order one day to be united to him.
>
> —St. Damien de Veuster

9
monday

Acts 19:1-8 • Ps 68:2-7b • Jn 16:29-33

_____
_____
_____
_____
_____
_____
_____
_____
_____

SAINT DAMIEN DE VEUSTER
Acts 20:17-27 • Ps 68:10-11, 20-21 • Jn 17:1-11a

10
tuesday

_____
_____
_____
_____
_____
_____
_____
_____
_____

> Look into my heart and see there the love and mercy
> which I have for humankind and especially for sinners.
> Look, and enter into my passion.
>
> —Jesus to St. Faustina (Diary 1663)

11
wednesday

Acts 20:28-38 • Ps 68:29-30, 33-36b • Jn 17:11b-19

_____
_____
_____
_____
_____
_____
_____
_____
_____

SAINTS NEREUS AND ACHILLEUS;
SAINT PANCRAS

Acts 22:30; 23:6-11 • Ps 16:1-2a, 5, 7-11 • Jn 17:20-26

12
thursday

_____
_____
_____
_____
_____
_____
_____
_____
_____
_____

May

The message of Fatima is, in its basic meaning, a call to conversion and repentance, as in the Gospel. . . . The call to repentance is a motherly one, and at the same time, it is strong and decisive.

—St. John Paul II

13
friday

OUR LADY OF FATIMA
Acts 25:13b-21 • Ps 103:1-2, 11-12, 19-20b
Jn 21:15-19

_____
_____
_____
_____
_____
_____
_____
_____
_____

SAINT MATTHIAS, APOSTLE
Acts 1:15-17, 20-26 • Ps 113:1-8 • Jn 15:9-17

14
saturday

_____
_____
_____
_____
_____
_____
_____
_____
_____
_____

> Rejoicing and eternal praise be to you, my Lord Jesus Christ,
> who sent the Holy Spirit into the hearts of your disciples.
>
> —St. Bridget of Sweden

15 sunday

PENTECOST SUNDAY
Acts 2:1-11 • Ps 104:1, 24, 29-31, 34 • 1 Cor 12:3b-7, 12-13 or Rom 8:8-17 • Jn 20:19-23 or Jn 14:15-16, 23b-26

(SEVENTH WEEK IN ORDINARY TIME)
Jas 3:13-18 • Ps 19:8-10, 15 • Mk 9:14-29

16 monday

May

> Mercy triumphs over judgment.

> —James 2:13

17
tuesday

Jas 4:1-10 • Ps 55:7-11a, 23 • Mk 9:30-37

_____

_____

_____

_____

_____

_____

_____

_____

_____

_____

SAINT JOHN I
Jas 4:13-17 • Ps 49:2-3, 6-11 • Mk 9:38-40

18
wednesday

_____

_____

_____

_____

_____

_____

_____

_____

_____

_____

The Name of Jesus is the most sweet-tasting nourishment
of contemplation, for it feeds and revives those souls
that are famished and spiritually hungry.

—St. Bernardine of Siena

19
thursday

Jas 5:1-6 • Ps 49:14-20 • Mk 9:41-50

_____

_____

_____

_____

_____

_____

_____

_____

_____

_____

SAINT BERNADINE OF SIENA
Jas 5:9-12 • Ps 103:1-4, 8-9, 11-12 • Mk 10:1-12

20
friday

_____

_____

_____

_____

_____

_____

_____

_____

_____

_____

May

> You, O Eternal Trinity, are a deep ocean, into which
> the more I penetrate, the more I discover, and the more
> I discover, the more I seek you.
>
> —St. Catherine of Siena

21 saturday — SAINT CHRISTOPHER MAGALLANES AND COMPANIONS

Jas 5:13-20 • Ps 141:1-3, 8 • Mk 10:13-16

THE MOST HOLY TRINITY

Prv 8:22-31 • Ps 8:4-9 • Rom 5:1-5 • Jn 16:12-15

22 sunday

I am plunged deep in mercies—I drown in them;
they cover me, wrapping me around every side.

—Blessed Charles de Foucauld

23
monday

(EIGHTH WEEK IN ORDINARY TIME)
1 Pt 1:3-9 • Ps 111:1-2, 5-6, 9-10 • Mk 10:17-27

1 Pt 1:10-16 • Ps 98:1-4 • Mk 10:28-31

24
tuesday

May

My Jesus, if you do not uphold me, I shall fall.
My Jesus, if you do not help me, I am ruined.

—St. Philip Neri

25
wednesday

**SAINT BEDE THE VENERABLE;
SAINT GREGORY VII; SAINT MARY
MAGDALENE DE' PAZZI**
1 Pt 1:18-25 • Ps 147:12-15, 19-20 • Mk 10:32-45

SAINT PHILIP NERI
1 Pt 2:2-5, 9-12 • Ps 100:2-5 • Mk 10:46-52

26
thursday

May mercy, peace, and love be yours in abundance.

—Jude 2

27
friday

SAINT AUGUSTINE OF CANTERBURY
1 Pt 4:7-13 • Ps 96:10-13 • Mk 11:11-26

_____
_____
_____
_____
_____
_____
_____
_____
_____

Jude 17, 20b-25 • Ps 63:2-6 • Mk 11:27-33

28
saturday

_____
_____
_____
_____
_____
_____
_____
_____
_____
_____

May

Jesus Christ instituted the adorable Sacrament of the Eucharist so that he might stay with us and be the Food of our soul; that he might stay with us and be our Companion.

—St. John Vianney

29
sunday

THE MOST HOLY BODY AND BLOOD OF CHRIST (CORPUS CHRISTI)
Gn 14:18-20 • Ps 110:1-4 • 1 Cor 11:23-26 • Lk 9:11b-17

_____
_____
_____
_____
_____
_____
_____
_____
_____
_____

(NINTH WEEK IN ORDINARY TIME)
2 Pt 1:2-7 • Ps 91:1-2, 14-16 • Mk 12:1-12

30
monday

_____
_____
_____
_____
_____
_____
_____
_____
_____
_____

By remembering the example of God's Mother,
we are encouraged to lead a life of virtue.

—St. Bede the Venerable

31
tuesday

THE VISITATION OF THE BLESSED VIRGIN MARY
Zep 3:14-18a or Rom 12:9-16 • (Ps) Is 12:2-6 • Lk 1:39-56

May

JUNE

Sun	Mon	Tue	Wed	Thu	Fri	Sat
			1	2	3	4
5	6	7	8	9	10	11
12	13	14	15	16	17	18
19	20	21	22	23	24	25
26	27	28	29	30		

The LORD is merciful and gracious,

slow to anger and abounding in steadfast love.

He will not always accuse,

nor will he keep his anger forever.

He does not deal with us according to our sins,

nor repay us according to our iniquities.

For as the heavens are high above the earth,

so great is his steadfast love

toward those who fear him;

as far as east is from west,

so far he *removes* our transgressions from us.

—*Psalm 103:8-12*

> For love of us God became man so as to
> share in our sufferings and heal us.
>
> —St. Justin

. . . .

1
wednesday

SAINT JUSTIN
2 Tm 1:1-3, 6-12 • Ps 123:1b-2 • Mk 12:18-27

_____

_____

_____

_____

_____

_____

_____

_____

_____

SAINTS MARCELLINUS AND PETER
2 Tm 2:8-15 • Ps 25:4-5b, 8-10, 14 • Mk 12:28-34

2
thursday

_____

_____

_____

_____

_____

_____

_____

_____

_____

[Jesus] has shown the face of God's mercy, and he has bent down to heal body and soul. . . . This is his heart which looks to all of us, to our sicknesses, to our sins. The love of Jesus is great.

—Pope Francis

3 friday — THE MOST SACRED HEART OF JESUS
Ez 34:11-16 • Ps 23:1-6 • Rom 5:5b-11 • Lk 15:3-7

THE IMMACULATE HEART OF THE BLESSED VIRGIN MARY
2 Tm 4:1-8 • Ps 71:8-9, 14-17, 22 • Lk 2:41-51

4 saturday

June

> Listen cheerfully to the word of God; keep it
> judiciously and observe it faithfully.
>
> —St. Norbert

5
sunday

TENTH SUNDAY IN ORDINARY TIME
1 Kgs 17:17-24 • Ps 30:2, 4-6, 11-13 • Gal 1:11-19
Lk 7:11-17

_____
_____
_____
_____
_____
_____
_____
_____
_____
_____

SAINT NORBERT
1 Kgs 17:1-6 • Ps 121:1b-8 • Mt 5:1-12

6
monday

_____
_____
_____
_____
_____
_____
_____
_____
_____
_____

You don't need to use many or high-sounding words. Just repeat often, "Lord, show me your mercy as you know best." Or, "God, come to my assistance."

—St. Macarius of Alexandria

7
tuesday

1 Kgs 17:7-16 • Ps 4:2-5, 7b-8 • Mt 5:13-16

_____

_____

_____

_____

_____

_____

_____

_____

_____

1 Kgs 18:20-39 • Ps 16:1b-2b, 4-5b, 8, 11 • Mt 5:17-19

8
wednesday

_____

_____

_____

_____

_____

_____

_____

_____

_____

June

Have mercy on me, O Lord, for you are abundant in mercy!
—St. Ephrem

9
thursday

SAINT EPHREM
1 Kgs 18:41-46 • Ps 65:10-13 • Mt 5:20-26

1 Kgs 19:9a, 11-16 • Ps 27:7-9, 13-14 • Mt 5:27-32

10
friday

Making the Father present as love and mercy is, in Christ's own consciousness, the fundamental touchstone of his mission as the Messiah.

—St. John Paul II

. . . .

11 saturday

SAINT BARNABAS, APOSTLE
Acts 11:21b-26; 13:1-3 • Ps 98:1-6 • Mt 5:33-37

_____
_____
_____
_____
_____
_____
_____
_____
_____
_____
_____

ELEVENTH SUNDAY IN ORDINARY TIME
2 Sm 12:7-10, 13 • Ps 32:1-2, 5, 7, 11 • Gal 2:16, 19-21 • Lk 7:36–8:3

12 sunday

_____
_____
_____
_____
_____
_____
_____
_____
_____
_____

June

. . . .

> O the mercy of God! Never does he refuse to be merciful,
> but is ever present to those who turn to him.
>
> —St. Anthony of Padua

13
monday

SAINT ANTHONY OF PADUA
1 Kgs 21:1-16 • Ps 5:2-7 • Mt 5:38-42

_____

_____

_____

_____

_____

_____

_____

_____

_____

_____

1 Kgs 21:17-29 • Ps 51:3-6b, 11, 16 • Mt 5:43-48

14
tuesday

_____

_____

_____

_____

_____

_____

_____

_____

_____

_____

> I believe that I shall be saved . . . for your mercy is
> greater than the malice of my sins.
>
> —St. Francis Xavier

15 wednesday

2 Kgs 2:1, 6-14 • Ps 31:20-21, 24 • Mt 6:1-6, 16-18

_____
_____
_____
_____
_____
_____
_____
_____
_____

Sir 48:1-14 • Ps 97:1-7 • Mt 6:7-15

16 thursday

_____
_____
_____
_____
_____
_____
_____
_____
_____

June

Lean on your Beloved, because the soul who abandons herself in the hands of Jesus in all she does, is carried in his arms.

—St. Clare

17
friday

2 Kgs 11:1-4, 9-18, 20 • Ps 132:11-14, 17-18
Mt 6:19-23

_____
_____
_____
_____
_____
_____
_____
_____
_____
_____

2 Chr 24:17-25 • Ps 89:4-5, 29-34 • Mt 6:24-34

18
saturday

_____
_____
_____
_____
_____
_____
_____
_____
_____
_____

Amazing grace! (how sweet the sound) / That sav'd a wretch like me! / I once was lost, / but now am found, / Was blind, but now I see.

—John Newton

19
sunday

TWELFTH SUNDAY IN ORDINARY TIME
Zec 12:10-11; 13:1 • Ps 63:2-6, 8-9 • Gal 3:26-29
Lk 9:18-24

_____
_____
_____
_____
_____
_____
_____
_____
_____
_____
_____

2 Kgs 17:5-8, 13-15a, 18 • Ps 60:3-5, 12-13 • Mt 7:1-5

20
monday

_____
_____
_____
_____
_____
_____
_____
_____
_____
_____

June

The precious blood of our Savior Jesus Christ
cries mercy for all sinners that do repent.

—St. John Fisher

21
tuesday

SAINT ALOYSIUS GONZAGA
2 Kgs 19:9b-11, 14-21, 31-35a, 36 • Ps 48:2-4, 10-11
Mt 7:6, 12-14

_____
_____
_____
_____
_____
_____
_____
_____
_____
_____

**SAINT PAULINUS OF NOLA; SAINTS JOHN
FISHER AND THOMAS MORE**
2 Kgs 22:8-13; 23:1-3 • Ps 119:33-37, 40 • Mt 7:15-20

22
wednesday

_____
_____
_____
_____
_____
_____
_____
_____
_____
_____

> "I tell you, among those born of women
> no one is greater than John; yet the least in the
> kingdom of God is greater than he."

—Luke 7:28

23
thursday

2 Kgs 24:8-17 • Ps 79:1b-5, 8-9 • Mt 7:21-29

_____
_____
_____
_____
_____
_____
_____
_____
_____
_____

THE NATIVITY OF SAINT JOHN THE BAPTIST
Is 49:1-6 • Ps 139:1b-3, 13-15 • Acts 13:22-26
Lk 1:57-66, 80

24
friday

_____
_____
_____
_____
_____
_____
_____
_____
_____
_____

June

The steadfast love of the LORD never ceases, / his mercies never come to an end; / they are new every morning; / great is your faithfulness.

—Lamentations 3:22-23

25 saturday

Lam 2:2, 10-14, 18-19 • Ps 74:1b-7, 20-21 • Mt 8:5-17

_____
_____
_____
_____
_____
_____
_____
_____
_____
_____

THIRTEENTH SUNDAY IN ORDINARY TIME
1 Kgs 19:16b, 19-21 • Ps 16:1-2, 5, 7-11 • Gal 5:1, 13-18 • Lk 9:51-62

26 sunday

_____
_____
_____
_____
_____
_____
_____
_____
_____
_____

> God did not make the first man because he needed company, but because he wanted someone to whom he could show his generosity and love.
>
> —St. Irenaeus

27
monday

SAINT CYRIL OF ALEXANDRIA
Am 2:6-10, 13-16 • Ps 50:16b-23 • Mt 8:18-22

_____
_____
_____
_____
_____
_____
_____
_____
_____
_____

SAINT IRENAEUS
Am 3:1-8; 4:11-12 • Ps 5:4b-8 • Mt 8:23-27

28
tuesday

_____
_____
_____
_____
_____
_____
_____
_____
_____
_____

June

We celebrate this day made holy for us by the apostles' blood. Let us embrace what they believed, their life, their labors, their sufferings, their preaching, and their confession of faith.

—St. Augustine

29
wednesday

SAINTS PETER AND PAUL, APOSTLES
Acts 12:1-11 • Ps 34:2-9 • 2 Tm 4:6-8, 17-18
Mt 16:13-19

_____

_____

_____

_____

_____

_____

_____

_____

_____

THE FIRST MARTYRS OF THE HOLY ROMAN CHURCH
Am 7:10-17 • Ps 19:8-11 • Mt 9:1-8

30
thursday

_____

_____

_____

_____

_____

_____

_____

_____

_____

In the mercy of God alone do we breathe.

—St. Bernard of Clairvaux

June

JULY

Sun	Mon	Tue	Wed	Thu	Fri	Sat
					1	2
3	4	5	6	7	8	9
10	11	12	13	14	15	16
17	18	19	20	21	22	23
24	25	26	27	28	29	30
31						

Let us be *renewed* by God's mercy, let

us be loved by Jesus, let us enable the power

of his love to *transform* our lives

too; and let us become agents of this mercy,

channels through which *God can*

water the earth, protect all creation, and

make *justice* and peace flourish.

—*Pope Francis,* Urbi et Orbi *Message,*
March 31, 2013

> All my life, I have . . . wanted to carry the gospel message to
> those who have never heard of God.
>
> —St. Junipero Serra

1
friday

SAINT JUNIPERO SERRA
Am 8:4-6, 9-12 • Ps 119:2, 10, 20, 30, 40, 131
Mt 9:9-13

_____
_____
_____
_____
_____
_____
_____
_____
_____

Am 9:11-15 • Ps 85:9ab, 10-14 • Mt 9:14-17

2
saturday

_____
_____
_____
_____
_____
_____
_____
_____
_____

> Teach me to feel another's woe, / To hide the fault I see; /
> That mercy I to others show, / That mercy show to me.
>
> —Alexander Pope

3
sunday

FOURTEENTH SUNDAY IN ORDINARY TIME
Is 66:10-14c • Ps 66:1-7, 16, 20 • Gal 6:14-18
Lk 10:1-12, 17-20

INDEPENDENCE DAY (USA)
Hos 2:16, 17c-18, 21-22 • Ps 145:2-9 • Mt 9:18-26

4
monday

July

> What is necessary, yes, I emphasize, necessary,
> is to have love—the love of God, the love that makes
> you pleasing to him.
>
> —St. Anthony Mary Zaccaria

5 tuesday
SAINT ANTHONY MARY ZACCARIA;
SAINT ELIZABETH OF PORTUGAL
Hos 8:4-7, 11-13 • Ps 115:3-10 • Mt 9:32-38

_____
_____
_____
_____
_____
_____
_____
_____
_____

SAINT MARIA GORETTI
Hos 10:1-3, 7-8, 12 • Ps 105:2-7 • Mt 10:1-7

6 wednesday

_____
_____
_____
_____
_____
_____
_____
_____
_____

> Have mercy on me, O God, / according to your steadfast love; / according to your abundant mercy / blot out my transgressions.
>
> —Psalm 51:1

7
thursday

Hos 11:1-4, 8e-9 • Ps 80:2-3b, 15-16 • Mt 10:7-15

_____
_____
_____
_____
_____
_____
_____
_____
_____

Hos 14:2-10 • Ps 51:3-4, 8-9, 12-14, 17 • Mt 10:16-23

8
friday

_____
_____
_____
_____
_____
_____
_____
_____
_____

July

> Martyrdom is the supreme witness given to the truth of the faith: it means bearing witness even unto death.
>
> —*Catechism of the Catholic Church,* 2473

9 saturday

SAINT AUGUSTINE ZHAO RONG AND COMPANIONS
Is 6:1-8 • Ps 93:1-2, 5 • Mt 10:24-33

FIFTEENTH SUNDAY IN ORDINARY TIME
Dt 30:10-14 • Ps 69:14, 17, 30-31, 33-34, 36-37 or 19:8-11 • Col 1:15-20 • Lk 10:25-37

10 sunday

> What is more delightful than this voice of the Lord calling to us? See how the Lord in his love shows us the way of life.
>
> —St. Benedict

11
monday

SAINT BENEDICT
Is 1:10-17 • Ps 50:8-9, 16b-17, 21, 23 • Mt 10:34–11:1

_____
_____
_____
_____
_____
_____
_____
_____
_____
_____

Is 7:1-9 • Ps 48:2-8 • Mt 11:20-24

12
tuesday

_____
_____
_____
_____
_____
_____
_____
_____
_____
_____

July

Present glory is fleeting and meaningless, while it is possessed,
unless in it we can glimpse something of heaven's eternity.

—St. Henry

13 wednesday SAINT HENRY
Is 10:5-7, 13b-16 • Ps 94:5-10, 14-15 • Mt 11:25-27

_____

_____

_____

_____

_____

_____

_____

_____

_____

SAINT KATERI TEKAKWITHA 14 thursday
Is 26:7-9, 12, 16-19 • Ps 102:13-21 • Mt 11:28-30

_____

_____

_____

_____

_____

_____

_____

_____

_____

> May Our Lady of Mount Carmel help us love
> nothing more than Christ.
>
> —St. John Paul II

15 friday

SAINT BONAVENTURE
Is 38:1-6, 21-22, 7-8 • (Ps) Is 38:10-12, 16 • Mt 12:1-8

_____
_____
_____
_____
_____
_____
_____
_____
_____

OUR LADY OF MOUNT CARMEL
Mi 2:1-5 • Ps 10:1-4, 7-8, 14 • Mt 12:14-21

16 saturday

_____
_____
_____
_____
_____
_____
_____
_____
_____

July

Grace, mercy, and peace from God the Father
and Christ Jesus our Lord.

—1 Timothy 1:2

17 sunday

SIXTEENTH SUNDAY IN ORDINARY TIME
Gn 18:1-10a • Ps 15:2-5 • Col 1:24-28 • Lk 10:38-42

_____
_____
_____
_____
_____
_____
_____
_____
_____
_____

SAINT CAMILLUS DE LELLIS
Mi 6:1-4, 6-8 • Ps 50:5-6, 8-9, 16b-17, 21, 23
Mt 12:38-42

18 monday

_____
_____
_____
_____
_____
_____
_____
_____
_____
_____

> Hear us, almighty Lord, show us your mercy;
> Sinners, we stand here before you.
>
> —Tenth Century Latin Hymn

19 tuesday

Mi 7:14-15, 18-20 • Ps 85:2-8 • Mt 12:46-50

_____
_____
_____
_____
_____
_____
_____
_____
_____
_____

SAINT APOLLINARIS
Jer 1:1, 4-10 • Ps 71:1-6b, 15, 17 • Mt 13:1-9

20 wednesday

_____
_____
_____
_____
_____
_____
_____
_____
_____
_____

July

> The Magdalene, most of all, is the model I like to follow. That boldness of hers, which would be so amazing if it weren't the boldness of a lover, won the heart of Jesus, and how it fascinates mine!
>
> —St. Thérèse of Lisieux

21 thursday

SAINT LAWRENCE OF BRINDISI
Jer 2:1-3, 7-8, 12-13 • Ps 36:6-11 • Mt 13:10-17

SAINT MARY MAGDALENE
Jer 3:14-17 • (Ps) Jer 31:10-13 • Jn 20:1-2, 11-18

22 friday

> O Lord God, forgive me my sins for the sake of your bitter
> pain and for your love of the human race.
>
> —St. Bridget of Sweden

23 saturday

SAINTS BRIDGET OF SWEDEN
Jer 7:1-11 • Ps 84:3-6a, 8a, 11 • Mt 13:24-30

SEVENTEENTH SUNDAY IN ORDINARY TIME
Gn 18:20-32 • Ps 138:1-3, 6-8 • Col 2:12-14 • Lk 11:1-13

24 sunday

July

Saints Joachim and Anna are a constant source of inspiration in everyday family and social life. Pass on to one another . . . the entire spiritual legacy of Christian life.

—St. John Paul II

25
monday

SAINT JAMES, APOSTLE
2 Cor 4:7-15 • Ps 126:1b-6 • Mt 20:20-28

_____
_____
_____
_____
_____
_____
_____
_____
_____
_____

SAINTS JOACHIM AND ANNE,
PARENTS OF THE BLESSED VIRGIN MARY
Jer 14:17-22 • Ps 79:8, 9, 11, 13 • Mt 13:36-43

26
tuesday

_____
_____
_____
_____
_____
_____
_____
_____
_____
_____

I praise God for his mercy; for it was he only who stretched
out his hand to me. May he be blessed forever!

—St. Teresa of Ávila

27 wednesday

Jer 15:10, 16-21 • Ps 59:2-4, 10-11, 17-18 • Mt 13:44-46

_____
_____
_____
_____
_____
_____
_____
_____
_____

Jer 18:1-6 • Ps 146:1b-6b • Mt 13:47-53

28 thursday

_____
_____
_____
_____
_____
_____
_____
_____
_____
_____

July

> You, Martha, if I may say so, are blessed for your good
> service, and for your labors you seek the reward of peace.
>
> —St. Augustine

29
friday

SAINT MARTHA
Jer 26:1-9 • Ps 69:5, 8-10, 14 • Jn 11:19-27
or Lk 10:38-42

_____
_____
_____
_____
_____
_____
_____
_____
_____
_____

SAINT PETER CHRYSOLOGUS
Jer 26:11-16, 24 • Ps 69:15-16, 30-31, 33-34
Mt 14:1-12

30
saturday

_____
_____
_____
_____
_____
_____
_____
_____
_____
_____

God's love for us is so great, so deep; it is an unfailing love,
one which always takes us by the hand and supports us,
lifts us up, and leads us on.

—Pope Francis

31
sunday

EIGHTEENTH SUNDAY IN ORDINARY TIME
Eccl 1:2; 2:21-23 • Ps 90:3-6, 12-14, 17 • Col 3:1-5,
9-11 • Lk 12:13-21

July

AUGUST

Sun	Mon	Tue	Wed	Thu	Fri	Sat
	1	2	3	4	5	6
7	8	9	10	11	12	13
14	15	16	17	18	19	20
21	22	23	24	25	26	27
28	29	30	31			

O Lord, we entreat your *goodness*

That you will forgive our sins,

And pass by our follies.

Open to us, O Lord,

The door of your tender mercies,

That there may come to us

Seasons of *refreshing,*

And if indeed, O Lord,

You open the door to the penitent,

In your *mercy* receive our petition!

—*St. Ephrem*

> Is our Lord not always the Good Shepherd, the Divine
> Consoler, the Changeless Friend?
>
> —St. Peter Julian Eymard

1
monday

SAINT ALPHONSUS LIGUORI
Jer 28:1-17 • Ps 119:29, 43, 79-80, 95, 102 • Mt 14:13-21

2
tuesday

**SAINT EUSEBIUS OF VERCELLI;
SAINT PETER JULIAN EYMARD**
Jer 30:1-2, 12-15, 18-22 • Ps 102:16-23, 29 • Mt 14:22-36 or Mt 15:1-2, 10-14

> Our sins are nothing but a grain of sand alongside
> the great mountain of the mercy of God.
>
> —St. John Vianney

3 wednesday

Jer 31:1-7 • (Ps) Jer 31:10-13 • Mt 15:21-28

_____
_____
_____
_____
_____
_____
_____
_____
_____
_____

SAINT JOHN VIANNEY
Jer 31:31-34 • Ps 51:12-15, 18-19 • Mt 16:13-23

4 thursday

_____
_____
_____
_____
_____
_____
_____
_____
_____
_____

August

> Our Lord allowed Peter, James, and John to enjoy for a very
> short time the contemplation of happiness that lasts forever
> so as to be able to bear adversity with greater fortitude.
>
> —St. Bede the Venerable

5
friday

**THE DEDICATION OF THE BASILICA
OF SAINT MARY MAJOR**
Na 2:1, 3; 3:1-3, 6-7 • (Ps) Dt 32:35c-36b, 39, 41
Mt 16:24-28

THE TRANSFIGURATION OF THE LORD
Dn 7:9-10, 13-14 • Ps 97:1-2, 5-6, 9 • 2 Pt 1:16-19
Lk 9:28b-36

6
saturday

> If you cannot weep for your own sins because you have none,
> still there are many sinners to be directed
> to God's mercy and love.
>
> —St. Dominic

7
sunday

NINETEENTH SUNDAY IN ORDINARY TIME
Wis 18:6-9 • Ps 33:1, 12, 18-22 • Heb 11:1-2, 8-19
Lk 12:32-48

SAINT DOMINIC
Ez 1:2-5, 24-28c • Ps 148:1-2, 11-14 • Mt 17:22-27

8
monday

August

Just take everything exactly as it is, put it in God's hands,
and leave it with him. Then you will be able to
rest in him—really rest.

—St. Teresa Benedicta of the Cross (Edith Stein)

9
tuesday

SAINT TERESA BENEDICTA OF THE CROSS (EDITH STEIN)
Ez 2:8–3:4 • Ps 119:14, 24, 72, 103, 111, 131
Mt 18:1-5, 10, 12-14

_____
_____
_____
_____
_____
_____
_____
_____
_____
_____

SAINT LAWRENCE
2 Cor 9:6-10 • Ps 112:1-2, 5-9 • Jn 12:24-26

10
wednesday

_____
_____
_____
_____
_____
_____
_____
_____
_____
_____

Look, look on Jesus, poor and crucified, look on this Holy
One, who for your love has died, and remember [that] . . .
this Jesus, whom you gaze upon, loves you most tenderly.

—St. Clare

11
thursday

SAINT CLARE
Ez 12:1-12 • Ps 78:56-59, 61-62 • Mt 18:21–19:1

SAINT JANE FRANCES DE CHANTAL
Ez 16:1-15, 60, 63 • (Ps) Is 12:2-6 • Mt 19:3-12

12
friday

August

Christ, like a skillful physician, understands the weakness of men. He loves to teach the ignorant, and the erring he turns again to his own true way.

—St. Hippolytus

SAINTS PONTIAN AND HIPPOLYTUS
13 saturday
Ez 18:1-10, 13b, 30-32 • Ps 51:12-15, 18-19
Mt 19:13-15

_____

_____

_____

_____

_____

_____

_____

_____

_____

_____

TWENTIETH SUNDAY IN ORDINARY TIME

14 sunday
Jer 38:4-6, 8-10 • Ps 40:2-4, 18 • Heb 12:1-4
Lk 12:49-53

_____

_____

_____

_____

_____

_____

_____

_____

_____

_____

The Assumption of the Blessed Virgin is a singular participation in her Son's resurrection and an anticipation of the resurrection of other Christians.

—*Catechism of the Catholic Church*, 966

15
monday

THE ASSUMPTION OF THE BLESSED VIRGIN MARY
Rv 11:19a; 12:1-6a, 10ab • Ps 45:10-12, 16 • 1 Cor 15:20-27 • Lk 1:39-56 • *Not a Holy Day of Obligation This Year*

SAINT STEPHEN OF HUNGARY
Ez 28:1-10 • (Ps) Dt 32:26-28, 30, 35c-36b
Mt 19:23-30

16
tuesday

August

God always thinks with mercy: do not forget this.
God always thinks mercifully. He is the merciful Father!

—Pope Francis

. . . .

17
wednesday

Ez 34:1-11 • Ps 23:1-6 • Mt 20:1-16

_____
_____
_____
_____
_____
_____
_____
_____
_____

Ez 36:23-28 • Ps 51:12-15, 18-19 • Mt 22:1-14

18
thursday

_____
_____
_____
_____
_____
_____
_____
_____
_____

This twofold mercy abounds in the heart of the Lord Jesus—
his long-suffering in waiting for the sinner and
his readiness in granting pardon.

—St. Bernard of Clairvaux

19 friday — SAINT JOHN EUDES
Ez 37:1-14 • Ps 107:2-9 • Mt 22:34-40

SAINT BERNARD — 20 saturday
Ez 43:1-7ab • Ps 85:9ab-14 • Mt 23:1-12

August

Because the Virgin Mary was raised to such a lofty dignity as to be the mother of the King of kings, it is deservedly and by every right that the Church has honored her with the title of "Queen."

—St. Alphonsus Liguori

21 sunday

TWENTY-FIRST SUNDAY IN ORDINARY TIME
Is 66:18-21 • Ps 117:1-2 • Heb 12:5-7, 11-13
Lk 13:22-30

THE QUEENSHIP OF THE BLESSED VIRGIN MARY
2 Thes 1:1-5, 11-12 • Ps 96:1-5 • Mt 23:13-22

22 monday

When we serve the poor and the sick, we serve Jesus. We must not fail to help our neighbors, because in them we serve Jesus.

—St. Rose of Lima

23 tuesday

SAINT ROSE OF LIMA
2 Thes 2:1-3a, 14-17 • Ps 96:10-13 • Mt 23:23-26

SAINT BARTHOLOMEW, APOSTLE
Rv 21:9ab-14 • Ps 145:10-13, 17-18 • Jn 1:45-51

24 wednesday

August

Be kindhearted to the poor, the unfortunate, and the afflicted.
Give them as much help and consolation as you can.

—St. Louis of France

25
thursday

SAINT LOUIS; SAINT JOSEPH CALASANZ
1 Cor 1:1-9 • Ps 145:2-7 • Mt 24:42-51

1 Cor 1:17-25 • Ps 33:1-2, 4-5, 10-11 • Mt 25:1-13

26
friday

> Our only hope, our only confidence, our only assured
> promise, Lord, is your mercy.
>
> —St. Augustine

27
saturday

SAINT MONICA
1 Cor 1:26-31 • Ps 33:12-13, 18-21 • Mt 25:14-30

_____
_____
_____
_____
_____
_____
_____
_____
_____
_____

TWENTY-SECOND SUNDAY IN
ORDINARY TIME

28
sunday

Sir 3:17-18, 20, 28-29 • Ps 68:4-7, 10-11 • Heb 12:18-
19, 22-24a • Lk 14:1, 7-14

_____
_____
_____
_____
_____
_____
_____
_____
_____
_____

August

By celebrating [John the Baptist's] birth and martyrdom, the Church unites herself to his desire: *He must increase, but I must decrease.*

—*Catechism of the Catholic Church,* 524

29 monday

THE PASSION OF SAINT JOHN THE BAPTIST
1 Cor 2:1-5 • Ps 119:97-102 • Mk 6:17-29

_____
_____
_____
_____
_____
_____
_____
_____
_____
_____

1 Cor 2:10b-16 • Ps 145:8-14 • Lk 4:31-37

30 tuesday

_____
_____
_____
_____
_____
_____
_____
_____
_____
_____

God alone is infinitely wise, holy, merciful, our Lord, Creator,
Father; he is beginning and end, wisdom and power
and love; he is all.

—St. Maximilian Mary Kolbe

31
wednesday

1 Cor 3:1-9 • Ps 33:12-15, 20-21 • Lk 4:38-44

August

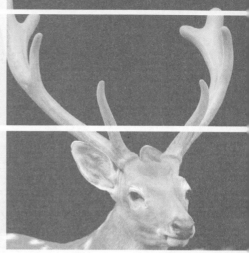

SEPTEMBER

Sun	Mon	Tue	Wed	Thu	Fri	Sat
				1	2	3
4	5	6	7	8	9	10
11	12	13	14	15	16	17
18	19	20	21	22	23	24
25	26	27	28	29	30	

No human sin can erase the

mercy of God or prevent him from

unleashing all his triumphant power,

if we only call upon him. *Indeed,* sin

itself makes even more radiant the love of the

Father. In order to *ransom* a slave, he

sacrificed his Son: his mercy

toward us is redemption.

—*St. John Paul II,* The Splendor of Truth, *118*

> Mercy . . . is a good thing, for it makes men perfect,
> in that it imitates the perfect Father. Nothing graces the
> Christian soul so much as mercy.
>
> —St. Ambrose

1 thursday

1 Cor 3:18-23 • Ps 24:1b-6 • Lk 5:1-11

1 Cor 4:1-5 • Ps 37:3-6, 27-28, 39-40 • Lk 5:33-39

2 friday

> Let us approach the throne of grace with boldness, so that we
> may receive mercy and find grace to help in time of need.
>
> —Hebrews 4:16

3 saturday

SAINT GREGORY THE GREAT
1 Cor 4:6b-15 • Ps 145:17-21 • Lk 6:1-5

_____

_____

_____

_____

_____

_____

_____

_____

_____

_____

TWENTY-THIRD SUNDAY IN ORDINARY TIME
Wis 9:13-18b • Ps 90:3-6, 12-17 • Phlm 9-10, 12-17
Lk 14:25-33

4 sunday

_____

_____

_____

_____

_____

_____

_____

_____

_____

_____

September

Christ comes to bring us the mercy of a God who saves. We are asked to trust in him, to correspond to the gift of his love with a good life, made up of actions motivated by faith and love.

—Pope Francis

. . . .

5
monday

LABOR DAY (USA)
1 Cor 5:1-8 • Ps 5:5-7, 12 • Lk 6:6-11

_____
_____
_____
_____
_____
_____
_____
_____
_____

1 Cor 6:1-11 • Ps 149:1b-6a, 9b • Lk 6:12-19

6
tuesday

_____
_____
_____
_____
_____
_____
_____
_____
_____

> We should be filled with joy at the birth of Mary. Her womb was a most holy temple. There, God received his human nature and thus entered visibly into the world of men.
>
> —St. Peter Damian

7
wednesday

1 Cor 7:25-31 • Ps 45:11-12, 14-17 • Lk 6:20-26

_____

_____

_____

_____

_____

_____

_____

_____

_____

THE NATIVITY OF THE BLESSED VIRGIN MARY
Mi 5:1-4a or Rom 8:28-30 • Ps 13:6 • Mt 1:1-16, 18-23

8
thursday

_____

_____

_____

_____

_____

_____

_____

_____

_____

_____

_____

September

Seek God in all things and we shall find God by our side.

—St. Peter Claver

9
friday

SAINT PETER CLAVER
1 Cor 9:16-19, 22b-27 • Ps 84:3-6, 12 • Lk 6:39-42

_____
_____
_____
_____
_____
_____
_____
_____
_____
_____

1 Cor 10:14-22 • Ps 116:12-13, 17-18 • Lk 6:43-49

10
saturday

_____
_____
_____
_____
_____
_____
_____
_____
_____
_____

O name of Mary! Joy in the heart, honey in the mouth,
melody in the ear of those devoted to her!

—St. Anthony of Padua

11
sunday

**TWENTY-FOURTH SUNDAY
IN ORDINARY TIME**
Ex 32:7-11, 13-14 • Ps 51:3-4, 12-13, 17, 19
1 Tm 1:12-17 • Lk 15:1-32

THE MOST HOLY NAME OF MARY
1 Cor 11:17-26, 33 • Ps 40:7-10, 17 • Lk 7:1-10

12
monday

September

The cross of Christ has become a source from
which flow rivers of living water.

—St. John Paul II

. . . .

13
tuesday

SAINT JOHN CHRYSOSTOM
1 Cor 12:12-14, 27-31a • Ps 100:1b-5 • Lk 7:11-17

_____
_____
_____
_____
_____
_____
_____
_____
_____
_____

THE EXALTATION OF THE HOLY CROSS
Nm 21:4b-9 • Ps 78:1b-2, 34-38 • Phil 2:6-11
Jn 3:13-17

14
wednesday

_____
_____
_____
_____
_____
_____
_____
_____
_____
_____

May she, who followed her Son with faith all the
way to Calvary, help us to walk behind him,
carrying his cross with serenity and love.

—Pope Francis

15 thursday

OUR LADY OF SORROWS
1 Cor 15:1-11 • Ps 118:1b-2, 16-17, 28 • Jn 19:25-27
or Lk 2:33-35

_____
_____
_____
_____
_____
_____
_____
_____
_____
_____

SAINTS CORNELIUS AND CYPRIAN
1 Cor 15:12-20 • Ps 17:1, 6-8, 15 • Lk 8:1-3

16 friday

_____
_____
_____
_____
_____
_____
_____
_____
_____
_____

September

> It is . . . necessary for us to get into the way of always
> and instinctively turning to God.
>
> —St. Robert Bellarmine

. . . .

17
saturday

SAINT ROBERT BELLARMINE
1 Cor 15:35-37, 42-49 • Ps 56:10c-14 • Lk 8:4-15

_____

_____

_____

_____

_____

_____

_____

_____

_____

_____

TWENTY-FIFTH SUNDAY IN ORDINARY TIME
Am 8:4-7 • Ps 113:1-2, 4-8 • 1 Tm 2:1-8 • Lk 16:1-13

18
sunday

_____

_____

_____

_____

_____

_____

_____

_____

_____

_____

> The Lord is like a farmer, and we are the field
> of rice that he fertilizes with his grace.
>
> —St. Andrew Kim Tae-gon

19
monday

SAINT JANUARIUS
Prv 3:27-34 • Ps 15:2-5 • Lk 8:16-18

_____
_____
_____
_____
_____
_____
_____
_____
_____
_____

SAINTS ANDREW KIM TAE-GON AND PAUL CHONG HA-SANG AND COMPANIONS
Prv 21:1-6, 10-13 • Ps 119:1, 27, 30, 34-35, 44
Lk 8:19-21

20
tuesday

_____
_____
_____
_____
_____
_____
_____
_____
_____
_____

September

Through his example and the words of his Gospel,
Saint Matthew constantly invites us to respond with
joy to the "good news" of God's saving mercy.

—Pope Benedict XVI

21
wednesday

SAINT MATTHEW, APOSTLE AND EVANGELIST
Eph 4:1-7, 11-13 • Ps 19:2-5 • Mt 9:9-13

Eccl 1:2-11 • Ps 90:3-6, 12-14, 17bc • Lk 9:7-9

22
thursday

> If the soul longs for nothing else than to love its God,
> then don't worry and be quite sure that this soul possesses
> everything, that it possesses God himself.
>
> —St. Pius (Pio) of Pietrelcina

23
friday

SAINT PIUS (PIO) OF PIETRELCINA
Eccl 3:1-11 • Ps 144:1b-4 • Lk 9:18-22

_____
_____
_____
_____
_____
_____
_____
_____
_____
_____

Eccl 11:9–12:8 • Ps 90:3-6, 12-14, 17 • Lk 9:43b-45

24
saturday

_____
_____
_____
_____
_____
_____
_____
_____
_____
_____

September

In what can I hope, then, or in whom ought I trust, save only
in the great mercy of God and the hope of heavenly grace?

—The Imitation of Christ

25
sunday

TWENTY-SIXTH SUNDAY IN ORDINARY TIME
Am 6:1a, 4-7 • Ps 146:7-10 • 1 Tm 6:11-16
Lk 16:19-31

SAINTS COSMAS AND DAMIAN
Jb 1:6-22 • Ps 17:1-3, 6-7 • Lk 9:46-50

26
monday

Extend mercy toward others, so that there is no one in need whom we meet without helping. For what hope is there for us if God should withdraw mercy from us?

—St. Vincent de Paul

27
tuesday

SAINT VINCENT DE PAUL
Jb 3:1-3, 11-17, 20-23 • Ps 88:2-8 • Lk 9:51-56

SAINT WENCESLAUS; SAINT LAWRENCE RUIZ AND COMPANIONS
Jb 9:1-12, 14-16 • Ps 88:10b-15 • Lk 9:57-62

28
wednesday

September

> Show me, O Lord, your mercy and delight my heart
> with it. Let me find you, whom I seek so longingly.
>
> —St. Jerome

29
thursday

SAINTS MICHAEL, GABRIEL, AND RAPHAEL, ARCHANGELS
Dn 7:9-10, 13-14 or Rv 12:7-12a • Ps 138:1-5 • Jn 1:47-51

_____

_____

_____

_____

_____

_____

_____

_____

_____

_____

SAINT JEROME
Jb 38:1, 12-21; 40:3-5 • Ps 139:1-3, 7-10, 13-14b
Lk 10:13-16

30
friday

_____

_____

_____

_____

_____

_____

_____

_____

_____

_____

[God] is the loving Father who always pardons,
who has that heart of mercy for us all.
And let us too learn to be merciful to everyone.

—Pope Francis

September

OCTOBER

Sun	Mon	Tue	Wed	Thu	Fri	Sat
						1
2	3	4	5	6	7	8
9	10	11	12	13	14	15
16	17	18	19	20	21	22
23	24	25	26	27	28	29
30	31					

The quality of mercy is not strain'd,

It droppeth as the *gentle* rain from heaven

Upon the place beneath: it is twice blest;

It *blesseth* him that gives and him that takes:

'Tis mightiest in the mightiest: it becomes

The *throned* monarch better than his crown;

His sceptre shows the force of temporal power,

The attribute to awe and *majesty*,

Wherein doth sit the dread and fear of kings;

But *mercy* is above this sceptred sway;

It is enthroned in the hearts of kings,

It is an *attribute* to God himself;

And earthly power doth then show likest God's

When mercy seasons justice.

—*William Shakespeare*, The Merchant of Venice

> I want only one thing: to begin to sing now what I will sing
> for all eternity—the mercies of the Lord.
>
> —St. Thérèse of Lisieux

1
saturday

SAINT THÉRÈSE OF THE CHILD JESUS
Jb 42:1-3, 5-6, 12-17 • Ps 119:66, 71, 75, 91, 125, 130
Lk 10:17-24

_____
_____
_____
_____
_____
_____
_____
_____
_____
_____

**TWENTY-SEVENTH SUNDAY IN
ORDINARY TIME**
Hb 1:2-3; 2:2-4 • Ps 95:1-2, 6-9 • 2 Tm 1:6-8, 13-14
Lk 17:5-10

2
sunday

_____
_____
_____
_____
_____
_____
_____
_____
_____
_____

Let us love God and adore him with pure heart and mind.
— St. Francis of Assisi

. . . .

3
monday

Gal 1:6-12 • Ps 111:1b-2, 7-10 • Lk 10:25-37

_____

_____

_____

_____

_____

_____

_____

_____

_____

_____

SAINT FRANCIS OF ASSISI
Gal 1:13-24 • Ps 139:1b-3, 13-15 • Lk 10:38-42

4
tuesday

_____

_____

_____

_____

_____

_____

_____

_____

_____

_____

October

Love God above all, so that warmed by his embrace
you may be aflame with divine love.

—St. Bruno

5
wednesday

Gal 2:1-2, 7-14 • Ps 117:1b-2 • Lk 11:1-4

_____
_____
_____
_____
_____
_____
_____
_____
_____
_____

**SAINT BRUNO; BLESSED MARIE ROSE
DUROCHER**
Gal 3:1-5 • (Ps) Lk 1:69-75 • Lk 11:5-13

6
thursday

_____
_____
_____
_____
_____
_____
_____
_____
_____
_____

> [Say] the Rosary, not simply with the lips, but with the attention of the soul to the divine truths, with a heart filled with love and gratitude.
>
> —St. John XXIII

7
friday

OUR LADY OF THE ROSARY
Gal 3:7-14 • Ps 111:1b-6 • Lk 11:15-26

_____
_____
_____
_____
_____
_____
_____
_____
_____
_____

Gal 3:22-29 • Ps 105:2-7 • Lk 11:27-28

8
saturday

_____
_____
_____
_____
_____
_____
_____
_____
_____
_____

October

To him who still remains in this world, no repentance is too late. The approach to God's mercy is open.

—St. Cyprian

9
sunday

TWENTY-EIGHTH SUNDAY IN ORDINARY TIME
2 Kgs 5:14-17 • Ps 98:1-4 • 2 Tm 2:8-13 • Lk 17:11-19

Gal 4:22-24, 26-27, 31–5:1 • Ps 113:1b-7 • Lk 11:29-32

10
monday

O give thanks to the LORD, for he is good; /
his steadfast love endures forever!

—Psalm 118:1

· ·

11
tuesday

Gal 5:1-6 • Ps 119:41, 43-45, 47-48 • Lk 11:37-41

_____
_____
_____
_____
_____
_____
_____
_____
_____

Gal 5:18-25 • Ps 1:1-4, 6 • Lk 11:42-46

12
wednesday

_____
_____
_____
_____
_____
_____
_____
_____

October

> O Jesus, my most sincere friend: come to my aid
> according to the magnitude of your mercies.
>
> —St. Margaret Mary Alacoque

13 thursday

Eph 1:1-10 • Ps 98:1-6 • Lk 11:47-54

_____
_____
_____
_____
_____
_____
_____
_____
_____

SAINT CALLISTUS I
Eph 1:11-14 • Ps 33:1-2, 4-5, 12-13 • Lk 12:1-7

14 friday

_____
_____
_____
_____
_____
_____
_____
_____
_____

His mercy is so great that he has forbidden none
to strive to come and drink from this fountain of life.
Blessed be he forever!

—St. Teresa of Ávila

15 saturday

SAINT TERESA OF JESUS
Eph 1:15-23 • Ps 8:2-7 • Lk 12:8-12

_____
_____
_____
_____
_____
_____
_____
_____
_____
_____

TWENTY-NINTH SUNDAY IN ORDINARY TIME
Ex 17:8-13 • Ps 121:1-8 • 2 Tm 3:14–4:2 • Lk 18:1-8

16 sunday

_____
_____
_____
_____
_____
_____
_____
_____
_____
_____

October

> He who died in place of us is the one object of my quest.
> He who rose for our sakes is my one desire.
>
> —St. Ignatius of Antioch

17
monday

SAINT IGNATIUS OF ANTIOCH
Eph 2:1-10 • Ps 100:1b-5 • Lk 12:13-21

_____
_____
_____
_____
_____
_____
_____
_____
_____
_____

SAINT LUKE, EVANGELIST
2 Tm 4:10-17b • Ps 145:10-13, 17-18 • Lk 10:1-9

18
tuesday

_____
_____
_____
_____
_____
_____
_____
_____
_____
_____

> My hope is in God, who does not need our help to accomplish his designs. We must endeavor to be faithful to him.
>
> —St. Isaac Jogues

- -

19
wednesday

SAINTS JOHN DE BRÉBEUF AND ISAAC JOGUES AND COMPANIONS
Eph 3:2-12 • (Ps) Is 12:2-6 • Lk 12:39-48

_____
_____
_____
_____
_____
_____
_____
_____
_____
_____

SAINT PAUL OF THE CROSS
Eph 3:14-21 • Ps 33:1-2, 4-5, 11-12, 18-19 • Lk 12:49-53

20
thursday

_____
_____
_____
_____
_____
_____
_____
_____
_____
_____

October

> Who can say that he is free from sin and
> does not need God's mercy?
>
> —St. John Paul II

21
friday

Eph 4:1-6 • Ps 24:1-6 • Lk 12:54-59

_____
_____
_____
_____
_____
_____
_____
_____
_____
_____

SAINT JOHN PAUL II
Eph 4:7-16 • Ps 122:1-5 • Lk 13:1-9

22
saturday

_____
_____
_____
_____
_____
_____
_____
_____
_____
_____

*My God, how good you are! How rich in mercy
you have been to me!*

—St. Anthony Mary Claret

23 sunday
THIRTIETH SUNDAY IN ORDINARY TIME
Sir 35:12-14, 16-18 • Ps 34:2-3, 17-19, 23
2 Tm 4:6-8, 16-18 • Lk 18:9-14

_____
_____
_____
_____
_____
_____
_____
_____
_____
_____

SAINT ANTHONY MARY CLARET
Eph 4:32–5:8 • Ps 1:1-4, 6 • Lk 13:10-17

24 monday

_____
_____
_____
_____
_____
_____
_____
_____
_____
_____

October

God, who is rich in mercy, out of the great love with which he loved us even when we were dead through our trespasses, made us alive together with Christ—by grace you have been saved.

—Ephesians 2:4-5

25
tuesday

Eph 5:21-33 • Ps 128:1-5 • Lk 13:18-21

_____
_____
_____
_____
_____
_____
_____
_____
_____

Eph 6:1-9 • Ps 145:10-14 • Lk 13:22-30

26
wednesday

_____
_____
_____
_____
_____
_____
_____
_____
_____
_____

May both Simon the Cananaean and Jude Thaddeus help us . . . to live the Christian faith without tiring, knowing how to bear a strong and at the same time peaceful witness to it.

—Pope Benedict XVI

27 thursday

Eph 6:10-20 • Ps 144:1-2, 9-10 • Lk 13:31-35

SAINTS SIMON AND JUDE, APOSTLES
Eph 2:19-22 • Ps 19:2-5 • Lk 6:12-16

28 friday

October

> God's mercy and grace give me hope
> —for myself, and for our world.
>
> —Billy Graham

29 saturday

Phil 1:18b-26 • Ps 42:2-3, 5 • Lk 14:1, 7-11

_____
_____
_____
_____
_____
_____
_____
_____
_____
_____

THIRTY-FIRST SUNDAY IN ORDINARY TIME

30 sunday

Wis 11:22–12:2 • Ps 145:1-2, 8-11, 13-14
2 Thes 1:11–2:2 • Lk 19:1-10

_____
_____
_____
_____
_____
_____
_____
_____
_____
_____

Let us be enveloped by the mercy of God; let us trust in his patience, which always gives us more time. Let us find the courage to return to his house, . . . allowing ourselves to be loved by him

—Pope Francis

31
monday

Phil 2:1-4 • Ps 131:1b-3 • Lk 14:12-14

October

NOVEMBER

Sun	Mon	Tue	Wed	Thu	Fri	Sat
		1	2	3	4	5
6	7	8	9	10	11	12
13	14	15	16	17	18	19
20	21	22	23	24	25	26
27	28	29	30			

You, O LORD, are a God

merciful and gracious,

slow to anger and abounding in

steadfast love and *faithfulness*.

Turn to me and be gracious to me;

give your *strength* to your servant.

—*Psalm 86:15-16*

> Follow the saints, because those who
> follow them will become saints.
>
> —St. Clement I

1 tuesday

ALL SAINTS
Rv 7:2-4, 9-14 • Ps 24:1b-6 • 1 Jn 3:1-3 • Mt 5:1-12a
Holy Day of Obligation

_____
_____
_____
_____
_____
_____
_____
_____
_____
_____

2 wednesday

**THE COMMEMORATION OF ALL THE
FAITHFUL DEPARTED (ALL SOULS' DAY)**
Wis 3:1-9 • Ps 23:1-6 • Rom 5:5-11 or 6:3-9 • Jn 6:37-40

_____
_____
_____
_____
_____
_____
_____
_____
_____
_____

> Behold Jesus Christ crucified. . . . His mercy is moved by
> the tears of sinners, and he never refuses pardon and grace to
> those who ask it with a truly contrite and humbled heart.
>
> —St. Charles Borromeo

3 thursday

SAINT MARTIN DE PORRES
Phil 3:3-8a • Ps 105:2-7 • Lk 15:1-10

_____
_____
_____
_____
_____
_____
_____
_____
_____
_____

SAINT CHARLES BORROMEO
Phil 3:17–4:1 • Ps 122:1-5 • Lk 16:1-8

4 friday

_____
_____
_____
_____
_____
_____
_____
_____
_____
_____
_____

November

> Love alone allows man to forget himself; . . . it alone can still redeem even the darkest hours of the past since it alone finds the courage to believe in the mercy of the holy God.
>
> —Karl Rahner

Phil 4:10-19 • Ps 112:1b-2, 5-6, 8-9 • Lk 16:9-15

5
saturday

_____
_____
_____
_____
_____
_____
_____
_____
_____
_____

THIRTY-SECOND SUNDAY IN ORDINARY TIME
2 Mc 7:1-2, 9-14 • Ps 17:1, 5-6, 8, 15 • 2 Thes 2:16–3:5
Lk 20:27-38

6
sunday

_____
_____
_____
_____
_____
_____
_____
_____
_____
_____

The mercy obtained through prayer will be like a torrent
coming from that immense ocean of the inexhaustible
goodness of the adorable heart of Jesus.

—St. Frances Xavier Cabrini

7
monday

Ti 1:1-9 • Ps 24:1b-6 • Lk 17:1-6

Ti 2:1-8, 11-14 • Ps 37:3-4, 18, 23, 27, 29 • Lk 17:7-10

8
tuesday

November

God wanted to set us free, and the way he
chose was to become one of us.

—St. Leo the Great

9
wednesday

THE DEDICATION OF THE LATERAN BASILICA
Ez 47:1-2, 8-9, 12 • Ps 46:2-3, 5-6, 8-9 • 1 Cor 3:9c-11,
16-17 • Jn 2:13-22

_____

_____

_____

_____

_____

_____

_____

_____

_____

SAINT LEO THE GREAT
Phlm 7-20 • Ps 146:7-10 • Lk 17:20-25

10
thursday

_____

_____

_____

_____

_____

_____

_____

_____

_____

> Grace, mercy, and peace will be with us from God the Father
> and from Jesus Christ, the Father's son, in truth and love.
>
> —2 John 3

11 friday
SAINT MARTIN OF TOURS
2 Jn 4-9 • Ps 119:1-2, 10-11, 17-18 • Lk 17:26-37

_____
_____
_____
_____
_____
_____
_____
_____
_____
_____

SAINT JOSAPHAT
3 Jn 5-8 • Ps 112:1-6 • Lk 18:1-8

12 saturday

_____
_____
_____
_____
_____
_____
_____
_____
_____
_____

November

O Jesus! . . . It did not suffice for you to take flesh, but you also wished to die! . . . O mercy! My heart drowns in thinking of you: for no matter where I turn to think, I find only mercy.

—St. Catherine of Siena

13 sunday

THIRTY-THIRD SUNDAY IN ORDINARY TIME
Mal 3:19-20a • Ps 98:5-9 • 2 Thes 3:7-12 • Lk 21:5-19

_____
_____
_____
_____
_____
_____
_____
_____
_____

Rv 1:1-4; 2:1-5 • Ps 1:1-4, 6 • Lk 18:35-43

14 monday

_____
_____
_____
_____
_____
_____
_____
_____
_____
_____

> O most sweet God of my life and the only love of my soul,
> your overabundance of mercy has led me through the many
> obstacles I have placed in the way of your love.
>
> —St. Gertrude

15
tuesday

SAINT ALBERT THE GREAT
Rv 3:1-6, 14-22 • Ps 15:2-5 • Lk 19:1-10

SAINT MARGARET OF SCOTLAND;
SAINT GERTRUDE
Rv 4:1-11 • Ps 150:1b-6 • Lk 19:11-28

16
wednesday

November

We cultivate a very small field for Christ but we love it, knowing that God does not require great achievements but a heart that holds back nothing for self.

—St. Rose Philippine Duchesne

17
thursday

SAINT ELIZABETH OF HUNGARY
Rv 5:1-10 • Ps 149:1b-6a, 9b • Lk 19:41-44

THE DEDICATION OF THE BASILICAS OF SAINTS PETER AND PAUL; SAINT ROSE PHILIPPINE DUCHESNE

18
friday

Rv 10:8-11 • Ps 119:14, 24, 72, 103, 111, 131 • Lk 19:45-48
(or for the memorial of the Dedication: • Acts 28:11-16, 30-31
Ps 98:1-6 • Mt 14:22-33)

> We have to affirm, with our words and with our deeds, that
> we aspire to make Christ the King reign over all hearts.
>
> —St. Josemaría Escrivá

19
saturday

Rv 11:4-12 • Ps 144:1-2, 9-10 • Lk 20:27-40

_____
_____
_____
_____
_____
_____
_____
_____
_____
_____

**OUR LORD JESUS CHRIST,
KING OF THE UNIVERSE**
2 Sm 5:1-3 • Ps 122:1-5 • Col 1:12-20 • Lk 23:35-43

20
sunday

_____
_____
_____
_____
_____
_____
_____
_____
_____

November

Let us ask Our Lady's help today in living our own dedication to the full, in whatever state God has placed us, in accordance with the specific vocation we have received from the Lord.

—Francis Fernandez

21 monday
THE PRESENTATION OF THE BLESSED VIRGIN MARY
Rv 14:1-3, 4b-5 • Ps 24:1b-6 • Lk 21:1-4

_____
_____
_____
_____
_____
_____
_____
_____
_____
_____

SAINT CECILIA
Rv 14:14-19 • Ps 96:10-13 • Lk 21:5-11

22 tuesday

_____
_____
_____
_____
_____
_____
_____
_____
_____
_____

Remember with thanksgiving the blessings and providence
of God . . . [and] glorify God, giving him from the
heart praises that rise on high.

—St. Anthony

23
wednesday

**SAINT CLEMENT I; SAINT COLUMBAN;
BLESSED MIGUEL AGUSTIN PRO**
Rv 15:1-4 • Ps 98:1-3b, 7-9 • Lk 21:12-19

**SAINT ANDREW DUNG-LAC AND
COMPANIONS; THANKSGIVING DAY (USA)**
Rv 18:1-2, 21-23; 19:1-3, 9a • Ps 100:1b-5
Lk 21:20-28

24
thursday

November

> Among the attributes of God, although they are all equal,
> mercy shines with even more brilliancy than justice.
>
> —Miguel de Cervantes

25
friday

SAINT CATHERINE OF ALEXANDRIA
Rv 20:1-4, 11–21:2 • Ps 84:3-6a, 8a • Lk 21:29-33

_____
_____
_____
_____
_____
_____
_____
_____
_____
_____

Rv 22:1-7 • Ps 95:1-7b • Lk 21:34-36

26
saturday

_____
_____
_____
_____
_____
_____
_____
_____
_____
_____

Mary sustains our journey toward Christmas, for she teaches us how to live this Advent season in expectation of the Lord.

—Pope Francis

27
sunday

FIRST SUNDAY OF ADVENT
Is 2:1-5 • Ps 122:1-9 • Rom 13:11-14 • Mt 24:37-44

Is 4:2-6 • Ps 122:1-9 • Mt 8:5-11

28
monday

November

Like [the apostle] Andrew, we too . . . have had an encounter
with the Savior and so understand more clearly the meaning
of the hope we are called to share with others.

—St. John Paul II

29
tuesday

Is 11:1-10 • Ps 72:1-2, 7-8, 12-13, 17 • Lk 10:21-24

_____

_____

_____

_____

_____

_____

_____

_____

_____

_____

SAINT ANDREW, APOSTLE
Rom 10:9-18 • Ps 19:8-11 • Mt 4:18-22

30
wednesday

_____

_____

_____

_____

_____

_____

_____

_____

_____

_____

Steep yourself in the meaning of these Advent days, and above all, pay heed to him who is approaching; . . . consider his purpose in coming, the ripeness of the times, the route he may choose for his approach.

—St. Bernard of Clairvaux

November

DECEMBER

Sun	Mon	Tue	Wed	Thu	Fri	Sat
				1	2	3
4	5	6	7	8	9	10
11	12	13	14	15	16	17
18	19	20	21	22	23	24
25	26	27	28	29	30	31

Awake, mankind! For your sake God has become man. . . . You would have suffered eternal death, had he not been born in time. Never would you have been *freed* from sinful flesh, had he not taken on himself the *likeness* of sinful flesh. You would have suffered everlasting unhappiness, had it not been for this *mercy*. You would never have returned to life, had he not shared your death. You would have been lost if he had not *hastened* to your aid. You would have perished, had he not come.

—*St. Augustine*

> We should always observe Advent with faith and love, offering praise and thanksgiving to the Father for the mercy and love he has shown us in this mystery.
>
> —St. Charles Borromeo

1 thursday

Is 26:1-6 • Ps 118:1, 8-9, 19-21, 25-27a • Mt 7:21, 24-27

_____
_____
_____
_____
_____
_____
_____
_____
_____
_____

Is 29:17-24 • Ps 27:1, 4, 13-14 • Mt 9:27-31

2 friday

_____
_____
_____
_____
_____
_____
_____
_____
_____
_____

God our Lord knows the intentions which he in his mercy has
wished to place in us, and the great hope and confidence which
he in his goodness has wished that we should have in him.

—St. Francis Xavier

3 saturday

SAINT FRANCIS XAVIER
Is 30:19-21, 23-26 • Ps 147:1-6 • Mt 9:35–10:1, 5a, 6-8

_____
_____
_____
_____
_____
_____
_____
_____
_____

4 sunday

SECOND SUNDAY OF ADVENT
Is 11:1-10 • Ps 72:1-2, 7-8, 12-13, 17 • Rom 15:4-9
Mt 3:1-12

_____
_____
_____
_____
_____
_____
_____
_____
_____

December

By contemplating our beautiful Immaculate Mother, let us also recognize our truest destiny, our deepest vocation: to be loved, to be transformed by love, to be transformed by the beauty of God.

—Pope Francis

5
monday

Is 35:1-10 • Ps 85:9-14 • Lk 5:17-26

_____
_____
_____
_____
_____
_____
_____
_____
_____

SAINT NICHOLAS
Is 40:1-11 • Ps 96:1-3, 10-13 • Mt 18:12-14

6
tuesday

_____
_____
_____
_____
_____
_____
_____
_____
_____
_____

> In Mary Immaculate we contemplate the reflection of
> the Beauty that saves the world: the beauty of God
> that shines on the face of Christ.
>
> —Pope Benedict XVI

7 wednesday

SAINT AMBROSE
Is 40:25-31 • Ps 103:1-4, 8, 10 • Mt 11:28-30

THE IMMACULATE CONCEPTION OF THE BLESSED VIRGIN MARY

8 thursday

Gn 3:9-15, 20 • Ps 98:1-4 • Eph 1:3-6, 11-12 • Lk 1:26-38
Holy Day of Obligation

December

I am a compassionate mother to you and to all of my devoted
children who will call upon me with confidence.

—Our Lady to St. Juan Diego

- -

9
friday

SAINT JUAN DIEGO CUAUHTLATOATZIN
Is 48:17-19 • Ps 1:1-4, 6 • Mt 11:16-19

_____

_____

_____

_____

_____

_____

_____

_____

_____

_____

Sir 48:1-4, 9-11 • Ps 80:2-3, 15-16, 18-19 • Mt 17:9a,
10-13

10
saturday

_____

_____

_____

_____

_____

_____

_____

_____

_____

_____

Hail, O Virgin of Guadalupe, Empress of America! Keep forever under your powerful patronage the purity and integrity of our holy Faith on the entire American continent.

—Pope Pius XII

11 sunday
THIRD SUNDAY OF ADVENT
Is 35:1-6a, 10 • Ps 146:6-10 • Jas 5:7-10 • Mt 11:2-11

OUR LADY OF GUADALUPE
Zec 2:14-17 or Rv 11:19a; 12:1-6a, 10ab
(Ps) Jdt 13:18b-19 • Lk 1:26-38 or Lk 1:39-47

12 monday

December

> The virgin comes walking, / the Word in her womb. / Could you not give her / a place in your room?
>
> —St. John of the Cross

13 tuesday

SAINT LUCY
Zep 3:1-2, 9-13 • Ps 34:2-3, 6-7, 17-19, 23
Mt 21:28-32

_____
_____
_____
_____
_____
_____
_____
_____
_____
_____

SAINT JOHN OF THE CROSS
Is 45:6b-8, 18, 21b-25 • Ps 85:9-14 • Lk 7:18b-23

14 wednesday

_____
_____
_____
_____
_____
_____
_____
_____
_____
_____

> May the mystery of the Incarnation of God in [Mary] be a
> source of joy and a stimulus for kindness, charity, and mercy.
> —St. John Paul II

15 thursday

Is 54:1-10 • Ps 30:2, 4-6, 11-13b • Lk 7:24-30

Is 56:1-3a, 6-8 • Ps 67:2-3, 5, 7-8 • Jn 5:33-36

16 friday

December

This time of Advent is a time of waiting for the Lord, who will visit us all on the feast, but also, each one, in our own hearts. The Lord is coming! Let us wait for him!

—Pope Francis

17 saturday

Gn 49:2, 8-10 • Ps 72:1-4b, 7-8, 17 • Mt 1:1-17

_____

_____

_____

_____

_____

_____

_____

_____

_____

_____

FOURTH SUNDAY OF ADVENT
Is 7:10-14 • Ps 24:1-6 • Rom 1:1-7 • Mt 1:18-24

18 sunday

_____

_____

_____

_____

_____

_____

_____

_____

_____

_____

Therefore the Lord himself will give you a sign. Look, the young
woman is with child and shall bear a son,
and shall name him Immanuel.

—Isaiah 7:14

19
monday

Jgs 13:2-7, 24-25a • Ps 71:3-6b, 16-17 • Lk 1:5-25

_____
_____
_____
_____
_____
_____
_____
_____
_____
_____

Is 7:10-14 • Ps 24:1-6 • Lk 1:26-38

20
tuesday

_____
_____
_____
_____
_____
_____
_____
_____
_____
_____

December

> The Virgin became pregnant with the Incarnation of Christ, may our hearts become pregnant with faith in Christ; she brought forth the Savior, may our souls bring forth salvation and praise.
>
> —St. Augustine

21
wednesday

SAINT PETER CANISIUS
Sg 2:8-14 or Zep 3:14-18a • Ps 33:2-3, 11-12, 20-21
Lk 1:39-45

_____
_____
_____
_____
_____
_____
_____
_____
_____
_____

1 Sm 1:24-28 • (Ps) 1 Sm 2:1, 4-8 • Lk 1:46-56

22
thursday

_____
_____
_____
_____
_____
_____
_____
_____
_____
_____

He who had his birth in Bethlehem came to be born in the hearts of men. For what would it profit us if he was born a thousand times in Bethlehem unless he was born again in man?

—Angelus Silesius

23
friday

SAINT JOHN OF KANTY
Mal 3:1-4, 23-24 • Ps 25:4-5b, 8-10, 14 • Lk 1:57-66

_____
_____
_____
_____
_____
_____
_____
_____
_____

2 Sm 7:1-5, 8b-12, 14a, 16 • Ps 89:2-5, 27, 29
Lk 1:67-79

24
saturday

_____
_____
_____
_____
_____
_____
_____
_____
_____

December

The Incarnation sprang from the goodness of God. The humility contained in this mystery is amazing, marvelous, astonishing. It shines forth with a dazzling brilliance.

—Blessed Charles de Foucauld

25
sunday

THE NATIVITY OF THE LORD (CHRISTMAS)
Is 52:7-10 • Ps 98:1-6 • Heb 1:1-6 • Jn 1:1-18

_____

_____

_____

_____

_____

_____

_____

_____

_____

_____

SAINT STEPHEN, THE FIRST MARTYR
Acts 6:8-10; 7:54-59 • Ps 31:3c-4, 6, 8ab, 16b-17
Mt 10:17-22

26
monday

_____

_____

_____

_____

_____

_____

_____

_____

_____

_____

The light shines in the darkness,
and the darkness has not overcome it.

—John 1:5

27 tuesday

SAINT JOHN, APOSTLE AND EVANGELIST
1 Jn 1:1-4 • Ps 97:1-2, 5-6, 11-12 • Jn 20:1a, 2-8

THE HOLY INNOCENTS
1 Jn 1:5–2:2 • Ps 124:2-5, 7c-8 • Mt 2:13-18

28 wednesday

December

> Our gaze on the Holy Family lets us . . . be drawn into
> the simplicity of the life they led in Nazareth. It is
> an example that does our families great good.
>
> —Pope Francis

29 thursday — SAINT THOMAS BECKET

1 Jn 2:3-11 • Ps 96:1-3, 5b-6 • Lk 2:22-35

_____

_____

_____

_____

_____

_____

_____

_____

_____

THE HOLY FAMILY OF JESUS, MARY, AND JOSEPH — 30 friday

Sir 3:2-6, 12-14 or Col 3:12-21 • Ps 128:1-5
Mt 2:13-15, 19-23

_____

_____

_____

_____

_____

_____

_____

_____

_____

> I go down on my knees before my God and,
> recalling his kindnesses to me this year, I humble
> myself in the dust and thank him with all my heart.
>
> —St. John XXIII

31 saturday

SAINT SYLVESTER I
1 Jn 2:18-21 • Ps 96:1-2, 11-13 • Jn 1:1-18

December

Reserve Next Year's *Prayer Journal* Today!

The Word Among Us *2017 Prayer Journal*

Continue your journey of faith with next year's *Prayer Journal*. As always, you'll get inspirational quotes and a complete listing of the daily Mass readings, saints' feast days, and holy days of obligation. Give it as a gift and introduce a friend to the pleasures of journaling.

—Also Available—

Abide in My Word 2017: Mass Readings at Your Fingertips

Keep abreast with the daily Mass readings and make personal Scripture reading easier! *Abide in My Word* provides each day's Scripture readings in an easy-to-locate format. Each day is clearly listed so that it only takes a few minutes to draw near to the Lord through the Mass readings. Use it together with your *Prayer Journal*.

To order, use the card below or call **1-800-775-9673**
You'll find up-to-date product information on our Web site at www.wau.org

Fill in the card below and mail in an envelope to:

The Word Among Us
7115 Guilford Drive, Suite 100
Frederick, MD 21704

Order 2 or more copies and save 20%!

- -

☐ **YES!** Send me _____ copies of the *2017 Prayer Journal*.   JP2017
   (1 @ $13.95; 2 or more @ $11.16 each plus shipping and handling)

☐ **YES!** Send me _____ copies of *Abide in My Word 2017*.   AB2017
   (1 *Abide in My Word* @ $16.50; 2 or more @ $13.20 each plus shipping and handling)

☐ **YES!** Send me the *2017 Prayer Journal* <u>AND</u> *2017 Abide in My Word* for only $24.36 plus shipping and handling!   17SETA

Name

Address

City

State   Zip

Phone (   )

E-mail (optional)

Send no money now. We will bill you.   VISA MasterCard DISCOVER

SHIPPING & HANDLING (Add to total product order):					
If your subtotal is:	$0-15	$16-$35	$36-50	$51-75	$76-100
Add shipping of:	$5	$7	$9	$11	$13

CPPJ16Z